WALKING
ON
Eggshells

Living with Psychological Abuse and Codependency

MCKENZIE BROWN

Order this book online at www.trafford.com
or email orders@trafford.com

Most Trafford titles are also available at major online book retailers.

Printed in the United States of America.

ISBN: 978-1-4669-5054-2 (sc)
ISBN: 978-1-4669-5053-5 (e)

Trafford rev. 07/28/2012

 www.trafford.com

North America & international
toll-free: 1 888 232 4444 (USA & Canada)
phone: 250 383 6864 ♦ fax: 812 355 4082

DEDICATED TO

You, who have sat alone in silent fear, the one who has kept the secrets of a loved one in order to do damage control. The one who escaped into their own cocoon, hoping the world would stop and make tomorrow a different day. The person who second-guesses everything they say or do for fear of rocking that dreaded boat. The one who works tirelessly to protect everyone but has no one to protect yourself.

Contents

"Codependency means," said one woman,
"that I am a caretaker."

PREFACE

I remember the first time I was told I was codependent as if it were yesterday. The room was dimly lit, with a drab sofa on one side and a small desk on the other. I was meeting my counselor for the first time, trapped inside the Calgary Women's Emergency Shelter. I argued with the counselor, explaining that I depended on no one. Everyone depended on me.

How had I ended up in such a place? I asked myself a thousand times. I was educated and had a high income. I travelled the world. I had loving parents. I raised four wonderful children. I owned a beautiful home and the perfect car. I was a good person.

I quickly learned that I wasn't a very good person to myself. Amidst those four dingy walls, my life was about to change forever. I quickly learned that being the caretaker was not always the best idea. That concept seemed so bizarre to me as I had been doing damage control from a young age on, always trying desperately to help my father and brother get along. That was my first recollection of being the caregiver, and that began in my preschool years. I could give you a list of my caretaking abilities that are a mile long, but I won't put you through it.

I was forty-two and found myself at rock bottom and had nowhere to turn except inside myself. I needed help, and I had for years; it just took this place for me to find it.

I want to share the story of how I ended up in that little space. I'm not sharing it out of vengeance or to try and redeem myself. I'm sharing this to help those who have walked that lonely marathon too. It felt like the chaos would never go away. I felt like dying. Out of that tiny counselor's room came a new light and, with that, a whole new life, but no one could have made me believe it the morning I stepped inside.

A year discussing my childhood and my present led me to understand how my life had gone from pink to black. More than that, it taught me how to go back to pink and far beyond. Without that time, I fear I would still be living in the dark chaotic world I had called my life, or perhaps I would have died.

My goal for this book is that it will be placed in the hands of every man or women entering a protective shelter. I really wish someone could have handed this to me the first day those cold steel doors crashed behind me. If you're that person, I want you to know you aren't alone, and this isn't your fault. I want you to understand that you can't help anyone until you help yourself. Most of all, I want you to see that life can be joyful again—a word that I had forgotten the meaning to at that time.

CHAPTER 1

The sun was shining, and it was beautiful when I met him,
then everything went crazy!

January 2008. It was cold winter day. Too cold to be outside, so I was bored. The house was clean, and there was nothing on TV. I wandered around my home in my flannel Mac's, wondering what to do. I just wanted to find something to do to get myself out of the pity party that had set in. My children were at their dad's, so I was all alone. I got this big idea to do an online dating profile. I had been divorced for several years and played the dating field, but I had not allowed myself to get very serious with anyone. So I thought I'd throw myself into the dating pool and see if God would send me a husband. That afternoon, even a buddy to hang out with would have been fun.

I must have gotten twenty-five e-mails the first day. The attention sure felt good. Having a good picture can really help with that. It was fun checking out the profiles and seeing what was available. A few of the guys that wrote me were pretty good-looking. I was impressed and wasted the next couple days glued to my computer, screening for potential dates.

I got an e-mail from this guy that wasn't very attractive, but his profile description intrigued me. It was about four paragraphs describing him as the ultimate giver. Being the good little codependent that I am,

I was impressed. I felt like I had been the giver my whole life, and it would be nice if someone would give to me for a change (not that the codependent in me would have ever given anyone a chance to give to me, but I had high hopes). In so many of my past relationships, I had been the one doing the work and paying the bills. So even though I wasn't at all attracted to the man claiming to be a giver, I gave him my msn user name.

I've always been pretty quick-witted, so he seemed to enjoy my jokes and smart-aleck remarks. I have to admit, I was chatting with about twelve different guys, and this one was the least attractive. He told me he was a personal trainer, and that impressed me too. Twenty years earlier, I had been really into fitness, working for a major sports team in my city. I had also just gotten back into the gym after taking a year off to recover from surgery and to eat nachos.

I had spent the summer before traipsing around Europe with my then eleven-year-old daughter Mandy and my amazing mother. We found some really great exercise machines there, and I was trying to have them built in China so I could sell them at home in Canada. Having another personal trainer's opinion on my plan seemed like good business sense, or I probably wouldn't have continued talking with him. He and I chatted and e-mailed throughout the day for a couple weeks.

I had been busy out meeting the good-looking ones on my list and didn't give my trainer much effort. He'd asked me out for coffee a few times, but I was never available because, like I said, I wasn't attracted to him, and in our e-mails, he didn't seem like the sharpest sandwich at the picnic. He had also told me that he was from Quebec. Growing up on a farm in Alberta, it was a God-given right of a conservative farmer's daughter to distrust anyone from Quebec. So before we met, he had seVernal points against him.

The phone rang early January 25. It was my personal trainer confirming our date for brunch. I had totally forgotten. Considering the fact that I had spent twelve hours dancing in four-inch heels the night before, who could blame me? I was out living the good life, and there might have been some red wine involved too.

I explained to him that brunch was out of the question. I looked like hell and felt worse. I wasn't going anywhere besides my comfy bed. He called back at noon and wanted to meet at a coffee shop near my home. I remember thinking *Jeez, buddy, go away.* I explained once again that I looked like crap and wanted to stay in. He told me that he wasn't coming to see how I looked as he had seen my picture and knew I could make myself look good, but he wanted to meet me and see what I was like on the inside. OK, so I was impressed. He told me to throw on a ball cap and just go have coffee. I can't believe I agreed, but I did just that! Typically, I would have spent an hour on my hair and makeup and slipped into something cute, but not for this date. I threw my hair into a ponytail and donned my favorite Boston Red Sox cap. To top it all off, I had to wear my daughter's winter boots because my feet hurt so bad from my night of dancing I couldn't get into my own. I was a sight but really didn't care. I was only planning to ask him if he knew what VibePlates were anyway.

We were supposed to meet thirty minutes after our call ended. He told me he'd be wearing a white ball cap. I casually waltzed into the coffee shop and sat down to wait. There was a guy in the corner with a white cap on, but he looked younger than forty-one and supergood-looking, so I knew he wasn't my guy. He was huge, like a bodybuilder or something. (I can pick out steroid users a mile away now but couldn't back then.) I remember smiling at him and thinking *Wow, what a pretty boy,* and looked away, wondering when my trainer would show up. Seconds later the bodybuilder in the white cap came to my table and asked if I was Mac.

If I could have known what I know now, I would have gotten up and walked out, but unfortunately, life doesn't work that way. I remember being shocked that this beauty was my trainer. I knew he would never ever date a girl like me, so I just decided to have fun, be myself, and laugh about it one day. I wasn't nervous even though he was the best-looking man I had ever seen. I was so positive he would never be into me that I never gave it much thought. He proceeded to give me his dating history (if you're single, make note of this). He told me how one girl after another had just screwed him over. He actually had tears in his eyes. I felt so bad for this huge victim I nearly gave him a hug in the middle of the coffee shop. His story was so sad. I recall thinking that he had met some real losers when, for the most part, the men from my past were awesome; some became my best friends and still are to this day.

We chatted for about ninety minutes, mostly about him, but he seemed to need someone to talk to, and I was a pro at that. I finally got up and left, knowing I'd never see him again. He'd answered my questions about my VibePlates, so I got what I came for. I had also gotten to spend an afternoon with the best-looking man I had ever seen, so for me, it was a win-win situation. I got in my little Honda and chuckled to myself, thinking that guy will never call. I mean, I was a forty-one-year-old grandma and twenty pounds overweight with a ball cap on.

I was just pulling out of the parking lot and still chuckling to myself, anxious to call my gal pal Ronnie and tell her this story, when my cell phone rang. Much to my surprise, he stunned me by asking to see me again two days later. Thank God there were no pedestrians because I would have run them over. I can't describe how it felt that someone so gorgeous could want to date me. Don't get me wrong; I usually land the better-looking ones, but this guy was in a class all by himself. Thinking back, I think I fell in love the very first day I laid eyes on him. I mean fireworks and the whole deal. This man needed me, and that fed my codependent nature like no one ever had.

I agreed to see him again. I then called my girlfriend Ronnie and asked her, "If I go home right now and get on my exercise bike and stay on it for two days, how much weight can I lose?" We still laugh about that phone call today. The sad part is, I did ride that stupid bike for about two hours a day. Pathetic, ay?

We met back at the coffee shop for coffee two days later as planned. No night of dancing or world plague could have stopped me. Only this time, I was looking as good as I possibly could. He must have thought I was someone different when I walked in. He never mentioned it though. We pretty much just talked about him again. I didn't mind because I was so nervous I could hardly speak anyway. I think Thumper once described what I was feeling as twitterpated.

He went on to tell me about his horrible life growing up with alcoholic parents and all the trials he had with his mother's awful boyfriends. He had tears once again as he spoke (single girls, make note of this too). I was so saddened to hear his story. I felt I'd had a pretty good life, growing up on a farm with two stable parents. My heart just ached for this man. He was so handsome I decided to name him Superman. As he spoke of his past, crying and blowing his nose, I remember putting my hand over his to try and comfort him. I just needed to help this poor man. I had so many breaks in life, and he hadn't. I believed I could help. (I wish I had known we can only help ourselves, but that lesson was yet to be learned.)

He offered to walk me to my car. I was impressed yet again and needed the help as I had been dumb enough to wear four-inch pumps in the ice and snow to try and impress this guy. He took my arm and escorted me to my car and asked if he could get in for a second. I didn't see any harm in that. I probably would have gone to city hall and married him at that point; I was so taken with him. I had never felt that way about anyone in my life, including my ex-husband of seventeen years. He was in my car all of sixty seconds, and he was kissing me—like making-out kissing. Gotta be honest here; he wasn't the best kisser I had ever kissed, but he was so pretty it didn't matter. Then he reached out and touched my breast. *Wow*, that brought me to my senses. I thought, *What nerve this guy has,* so I stopped him. He laughed about it, told me he was checking to see if they were real. I was rather busty back then, but not anymore. So I laughed too. He always had the ability to explain himself out of anything, and I always believed what he said. Thinking back, he was always a pro at justifying everything.

We'd dated a few times, so finally, I got the nerve up to ask him over for dinner. He wanted to go out, but the Super Bowl was on, and my Patriots were playing, so I wasn't missing that. I was a huge sports fan, and certain games or races couldn't be missed. I have a fifty-two-inch TV in my bedroom to prove my obsession. I often look back and wonder at what point did I let all my needs be thrown aside, but at that point, I still allowed myself whatever pleasured me.

I cooked Mexican food, and he was impressed. He ate like a small horse and went on and on about how good my cooking was. Of course, I was thrilled. We made out on the couch during game breaks, but eventually, the game ended, and it was time for him to go. He wanted to spend the night. I remember laughing and telling him "No way, José." I knew I never slept with anyone I wasn't in love with, and even though I was crazy about him, I just wasn't ready. He said that impressed him, and off he went. I am assuming, with his pretty face, most girls hopped into bed at his first request, but not me. I will, however, admit to a cold shower after he left.

CHAPTER 2

Relationships are like a dance, with visible energy racing back and forth between the partners. Some relationships are the slow, dark, dance of death.

—Colette Dowling

It was Valentine's Day, and we'd been dating for about three weeks. We were going for dinner. He hadn't made reservations until late, so we went to a little Italian restaurant not far from my home. I turned down a few other men that had planned romantic evenings because I already knew he was the one I wanted to be with. He came to my door looking as amazing as ever. As I watched him come up my front steps, I noticed he had a red carnation in his hand. I thought, *Wow, he's so sweet!*

No one had given me flowers in maybe ten years. Then he came inside and gave the flower to my daughter for babysitting my son so he could take me out. I'm such a sap that I will never ever forget that. He ordered the meal and picked out my favorite wine. I sat there in my best red dress. OK, it was new; I admit it. I listened to him talk for hours. He was back in tears again, telling me about his past girlfriends and how horrible they had all been. Again, I was feeling just terrible for him. There were no compliments for me and my new red dress, but it didn't matter; this poor guy was so filled with hurt that it just needed to be about him. Wiping his nose on his dress shirt, he asked me to rescue him with his eyes filled with tears. Codependents are born to rescue, so naturally, I was up for the task before I was even asked.

It was that night I met his best—and only—friend Tom. We went to the airport to pick him up from a Caribbean vacation. I remember liking him instantly, as in attracted to him. (I have never told anyone but Mandy about that). He actually asked some questions about me and seemed to give me a chance to talk. It was pretty cool and so was he. He was very funny and quick-witted and much more intelligent than my Valentine. I was totally taken with him. I felt guilty about that because I knew my new beau needed me to rescue him; Tom didn't. Tom told me that he had been on the dating website too, and I wondered how I had missed him. I wish I knew then what I know now. A smart girl would have picked Tom over my victim of a boyfriend any day.

My new man started training me at the gym a few days later. I was nervous and reluctant but finally agreed to let him be my personal trainer. There was very little warm-up and a ton of leg work. I wasn't going to admit that the weights were too heavy because I so desperately wanted him to like me. Looking back, I have asked myself why I worshipped him so much. I still can't answer that. Surely, it wasn't just because he was good-looking. I didn't know I was codependent or even what the word meant. He rarely let me talk about myself and almost never complimented me on anything. It was months before he even knew what I did for a living. I wonder if he really knows to this day.

After our first workout, he put me on a treadmill for thirty minutes and leaned on the front, chatting to me. I was so twitterpated, I'm surprised I didn't go scooting off the back. He would look so deeply into my eyes that I swear he could see right into my soul. Just his presence seemed to move me. It was that day on the treadmill when he asked me to be his girlfriend and remove my profile from the dating site. I couldn't feel my legs from the heavy workout, but I was the happiest girl in the world! I cranked the radio on the way home when the song "Bubbly" came on and sang all the way home. I was dancing on the ceiling. I was officially dating the greatest man in the world, and I was happy, very, very happy.

Two weeks later, I woke up in my bed next to Superman. I rolled over and watched him sleep. He was so beautiful, and I was so at peace.

His huge golden muscles were basking in the morning sunshine. I smiled thinking I had my own personal Greek statue. I got up and made him breakfast in bed. I think I had only done that maybe three times in my whole life, but only the best would do for my man. In honesty, the sex wasn't so great. It wasn't passionate and loving at all. Kind of rough and gross and lasted for maybe ten minutes, but I just assumed it was awkward because it was the first time. But he loved the breakfast-in-bed part, so I was thrilled. I was rescuing him just like I had promised I'd do, and that fed my codependency. I remember him thanking me over and over for breakfast. Oh, how I loved that; it made up for the crumby sex and then some. Still to this day, he was the most grateful man I ever met. Never once did he leave my side without saying "Thank you," something the men of my past didn't do. That impacted me. It fed me. I was positive that I was rescuing him already.

Very quickly, he started staying over every time my kids were with their dad, which were Tuesdays, Thursdays, and every other weekend. He usually got to my house pretty late because his work as a trainer kept him out until ten o'clock sometimes. I'd always have dinner ready at any hour he needed to be fed. After a while, I resented that but didn't have the guts to say anything and risk losing him at that point. He always got his breakfast in bed too. We'd eat in my bed and watch the news together. I miss that part and maybe always will. The sex didn't improve; in fact, it got worse. I remember during one session he called me his whore and some nasty stuff and pulled my hair. Don't get me wrong; I can get down with the best of them. In fact, I love it, but it was every time. At some point, I wanted the loving, passionate lovemaking session that every female requires. Never once did that happen.

Then one early morning, he decided he wanted anal sex. I hated every second of it. Good lord that hurt. I would never have let someone cause me such pain, but once again, nothing was too good for my trainer. If he wanted a porn star, I would perform. I faked that I liked it (this is one of those "God I'm an idiot" moments). I usually faked the orgasms too. We codependents will sacrifice ourselves on a daily basis if we think we can make someone happy.

Training with him was pretty awful. At night, I would put ice on my legs and cry because my quads hurt so badly. One night I slept on the coach because it hurt too bad to climb the stairs to my bed. I wanted to quit training with him; it caused so much pain. I came close to telling him, but that was the day he slapped my butt and said, "We are going to get this into the best shape it's ever been." My feelings were pretty hurt because men typically liked my butt, but it gave me the willpower to keep training with him day in and day out, sometimes for hours. In the gym, he was like an army sergeant at a boot camp. It was hell, but I never once complained. We were together pretty much every day from very early in the relationship. It's like he became my whole world or, shall we say, took over my world. My happiness and self-worth were starting to fade, but I ignored it because I was on a rescue mission.

My trainer never was much for compliments. I needed some, but they never came from him. Once in a while, he'd say I was smart or amazing but never pretty or, better yet, beautiful. Thinking back, I doubt he ever thought of me as that; I will never know. After a while, my confidence started to fade. I have since learned that some people who feel bad about themselves need to put those around them down so they can keep you. That was starting to work well for my Superman. Once the girl confident enough to don a baseball cap and head out for a date, I was now second-guessing everything about myself. The great eggshell walk had begun, and I never even noticed.

We'd only been together a few months, but I had already put my needs on a shelf to try and make him happy—the classic codependent that I am. I can actually only recall him being happy four times in that year. In general, he was grumpy, sad, miserable, and depressed, and he kept throwing temper tantrums.

I remember one time my mom phoned me and asked if I had ever seen him smile. My mother was my best friend. We talked daily, and already she was starting to worry about my changing attitude. My mom was the first to notice something was wrong.

I was ticked off at her, but she did have a good point. I would wake him with his plate of breakfast, and typically, the first word out of his mouth was *fuck*. Ya know I hated that. I was a morning person and worked hard to make his breakfast. You'd think just once he could have woke up with a smile. I tried to ignore that and, for the most part, did a pretty good job because I was going to rescue him and make him so happy he would forget grumpy and just love me. Food seemed to be my best bet. If he were full, he would thank me and tell me he loved me and, even better yet, that he needed me.

We used to send text messages all day, and we'd say the all this corny "I love you, Superman" and "You're my princess" stuff back and forth. Like ten and twenty times a day. I never saw it as obsessive at the time. I loved it, and it made me happy. Now so many years later, when my cell phone buzzes with a text message, I shudder; but I will get into that part later.

For the most part, I was pretty happy from January to April. Superman was a powerlifter. I believed that's why he had such a large body. He was a world champion in fact. He decided I was going to be a powerlifter too. I remember thinking he was crazy. I had always been very tiny and anything but strong. I didn't take it very seriously, but if he was happy, so was I. We had started training for my first powerlifting meet together in March, but then I had to leave for China in April, so my training was impacted. I didn't really care since he was the powerlifter, not me. I was gone about twenty-four days. It was weird; I hardly missed him and only called him a few times. A couple girlfriends had joined me on my trip, and we really had some fun. I enjoyed the rest from his bad moods and negativity and just got into work mode, which was the positive, happy me. My girlfriends had a few comments about my phone calls with him as we just seemed to talk about him. I ignored them, knowing he was a mess without me there and he needed me home. At some point, I already held myself responsible for his behavior. In honesty, that made me feel good. I called once after we got trapped in a typhoon and had some trouble with the Chinese military. Here's my journal entry from that day:

April 23

Called superman tonight from Guangzhou to tell him I made it back into china from Macau. He was upset and wants me home then went on about how he hates his client Glenda that never shows up, and how Tom is a big suck. Sometimes he sure doesn't talk very nice about the people that care about him. I sure hope he never does that about me. Called Vern . . . he made me feel better and encouraged me that I was going to be ok. I wonder when my superman will take 5 seconds to be about me. I will pray for him tonight as it sure seems he has the worst luck. Gotta sleep so tired. Big trade show tomorrow.

I was glad to get back from China. That was the one and only time he bought me flowers. He picked up my daughter Mandy and brought her to the airport. He forgot the flowers in the truck but just showing up meant the world to me. It made up for all the grumpy days. He owned me, and I truly believed I could help with all his sadness. It didn't take much to make me really happy. I started sending him e-mails of encouragement telling him how amazing he was every day. I thought it would help with his depression, which I had quickly learned was his middle name.

Then we trained hard for the nationals, my first ever powerlifting meet. I was doing bench press only. My Superman was doing all three lifts and so was Tom. It was then I learned about the steroids. My friend Klaus had tried to tell me that my Superman was on steroids, but I refused to believe it. When I asked him about it, he said he had tried them when he was young. Then he said he tried them a few years ago, and then he said he did them every so often. Then I learned he was doing a cycle as we trained for the meet and that he was shooting up Tom with them too. I was pretty disgusted as the story kept changing. The truth turned out that he was a regular user for twenty years.

I started researching them online and knew they were illegal but wasn't too concerned. I knew a few guys who had used them when I had been a trainer in football in my younger days. I had another friend's husband who did them a lot too, so I tried to just put it out of my mind. I just wanted to focus on my meet. I couldn't actually believe I was going on a stage to bench press. Keep in mind I'm five foot two and didn't really fit in with the big people of the gym. I was pretty excited. And to be allowed to do something with the man of my dreams was well beyond all my happiest thoughts. Superman wanted me to take some steroids too. I was actually stupid enough to go ask my doctor for his opinion. Even when my doctor said absolutely no way and had explained why, Superman pushed me hard to join him in his testosterone buffet of pills and injections. Luckily, I stayed strong and refused, promising to make it up to him. I made it up to him by tolerating the worst sex of my life. He'd call me terrible names and kind of slap me around, not painfully, but sex was really not fun at all. Little Ms. Codependent was willing to do whatever he wanted to make him happy.

My journal entry two days before the meet:

> *Dear dad* [sometimes I write my journal to my dad who had passed away],
>
> *I wish you were here. In two days I'm going to be bench pressing at a powerlifting meet. It's weird to think of doing it without you. I have worked so hard training for this. Some days my body aches so bad. Oh dad I'm happy. I wish you could have met this guy. He needs a dad like you. He didn't have a good dad by the sounds of things, but he will be ok he just needs to be loved and you taught me well on how to do that. Miss you, P.*

My journal entry the night before:

> *Holy crap I had a horrible day. I didn't know what weigh in was for the meet and my superman yelled at me like I was stupid. He was so mean. I should have been working on getting into a weight class that suits my lift but had no idea how all that worked. He only thinks of himself and no one else. He's a walking pity party. He*

is in a terrible mood. I have seen him down and grumpy but today he actually scared the heck out of me. He started honking at traffic on the way to weigh in and screaming and yelling at other cars. Then he asked if I knew where to go and all I said was take the next left. He freaked yelling at me saying "you fucking know everything your just a know it all and that I know more then everyone" and pretty much just repeated that for about 10 minutes. He was screaming at me because I gave him directions. He put his hand on my face and squished my head into the passenger side window. It hurt so bad. It felt like he was going to crush my skull. It still hurts to touch tonight. I'm shocked and confused. I was terrified as he screamed he drove faster. I wanted to curl into a ball and die. No one had ever talked to me that way. Who is this man? Then at 8:30 tonight he said I need spandex shorts. I had to run out and get them before the store closed in a panic. I am not in game mode at all just freaked . . . who is this man I love so much? Today he acted like a Monster, don't understand what is going on. I think we might be broke up but not sure . . . he's just really, really mad but don't know why. He actually scared me today. Why is this happening I have tried everything to be good to him. I'm scared about tomorrow, and scared of him.

Needless to say, my first meet was one of my more horrific experiences up to that day. He picked me up early but was even more grumpy than normal. I had packed a cooler of food, hoping if he ate he'd stop being so nasty. That normally worked. He was just foul, every second word was *fuck*, and I felt like a pain in his side. My heart was broken. I knew better than to speak as no matter what I said, it would be wrong. I sat backstage, so confused. I was truly walking on eggshells. Abuse victims learn quickly to shut up for fear of being hurt or, worse yet, causing a scene. It should have been an awesome day as I had trained so hard, but instead, I sat silently, only moving when he needed something from me. He crabbed and complained about everyone that needed his help. I know now it was his job to help, and it should have been an honor to aid his clients at a big meet like the nationals, but somewhere, logic had become clouded with my pity for my poor Superman. I thought it best to just be silent and do only what I was told and not move unless I was instructed to. Tread lightly and maybe he would forget I was there, and I wouldn't get some nasty comment or, my personal favorite, get the retard face he would make if I asked a stupid question or any question for that matter. I learned that day how to make myself disappear in a crowded room.

I ran into an old friend from the airline I used to work for; she was a lifter too. A pretty girl and a superstrong powerlifter. I was happy to see a familiar face. My Superman asked me how I knew her and explained. Then he told me that he had slept with her twice. I thought, *Oh, a girl he dated that didn't screw him over,* but he corrected that, saying she was not running on a full deck, and she was a fuck because he hadn't had any in a while. I was pretty disgusted with such a pig. I knew her, and she was nice. No one deserves to be used—well, except for me, Little Ms. Codependent; you can use me at will.

Much to my surprise, I made my lift and won a gold medal. I had never won a medal for anything in my life, and I was hooked on powerlifting. Thinking back to my early days, I became a trainer because maybe I could help an athlete win a medal seeing as I couldn't. That very day, I learned that no matter how tough life was, I had strength and no one—I mean no one—was going to take that away from me. Powerlifting was about me and no one else. It had empowered me like nothing ever had. I thanked him and gave him all the credit. He agreed that I would have never won if he hadn't trained me. Only he could make me into something to be proud of and no one else. He was responsible for everything good I did, and I should be thankful, just like Tom and all his clients. We were all nothing without him.

My Superman was in a crappy mood when we came home even though we had both qualified for worlds, but even his grumpiness couldn't bring me down. This time, I rolled him over and fucked his brains out. I would pulled his hair too if he'd had any. I was on cloud nine, but it had nothing to do with him, who had just gone from my Superman to Mr. Grumpy Pants. The nickname I had given him when we met was gone from my eyes the moment he freaked out in the truck. I didn't deserve to be yelled at or swore at, but he explained that he was just stressed about the meet. Thinking back, I know that was no excuse to scare someone, but that day, everything started to change for me. I certainly didn't view his behavior as abuse, but I really didn't like it either. Abuse to me was when someone hit you. He had laid hands on me but just to squish my head, not punch me, so it wasn't abuse. I imagine you would understand if you were sitting in a shelter, reading this.

About two days later, he and I were in line at a Tim Hortons near my house. He was one bear of a man. I sat silently as we waited in line at the drive-through. He wanted a coffee before we went to the gym to work out. The lady in front of us was taking too long. I hadn't really thought she was too long, but he got madder by the minute. Then he lay on his horn. I crouched down, embarrassed that he was doing that. It was so unjustified, and he was yelling out the window and swearing. I wanted to crawl under the seat. Then he threw the truck into drive and went right over the curb and left the drive-through line, mad as hell because the line was too slow. I knew instantly to be silent. His temper was out of control. Worse than anything I had witnessed, aside from when I gave him directions the week before.

We went to the gym without his coffee. I stayed silent. He was acting so crazy, I think I was in shock. Someone had slid a weight bench close to another one, and he picked up one end and tossed it across the gym floor. It scared the hell out of me. People were staring at us. I was so ashamed. One of his clients came up to me at the water fountain and asked if I was OK. I felt a lump form in my throat when he asked but held back the tears and said, "Oh yeah, he's just having a bad day." I was covering for him and didn't realize it; keep the peace and try to do damage control was all I could think of. I wish I had said, "No, I'm not OK. He's scaring me." Keep in mind, my trainer was 235 pounds of muscle, and I was about 135 pounds of nothing other than nachos. I will say that client of his has been a huge support to me at that gym since that crazy day. One day, I will hug him and thank him for offering me some support that day as I was so freaked out. He still smiles and says hello, asking me how I'm doing with concern on his face.

I didn't understand how my Mr. Grumpy Pants had gotten so out of control, but I began to do my research. That was when I learned about roid rage. For a long time, I blamed the steroids for his bad behavior. I'm sure they played a part, but that being said, I know a ton of steroid users who have strong emotions but act nothing like he did. I tried talking to him about it, but he said he would only be on the steroids until his strongman competition in June and then go off. I, being an idiot, actually believed him. He'd been using them for twenty years, but somehow, I believed he would just quit for our amazing love. If I sound bitter, it's because I am. That being said, Tom had been taking some steroids but was still as happy and funny as ever. Training for the strongman competition was long and hard. I wasn't competing, but he pushed me harder than ever at the gym. I learned to do whatever I was told no matter how great the pain.

His mood swings were almost daily, and it exhausted me. I was getting grumpy and fed up too. I resented everything, from the bad sex to making his breakfast, to only have him say *fuck* when I wake him up. By this time, I was paying for just about everything. He was broke and actually had to borrow money to pay his rent. However, he did pay me back every dime and continued to send really sweet texts. I have no idea why I stayed. Somehow, I knew he was the only man that would ever love me, and this was as good as life could get for me. His mental manipulation was taking its toll. My life was getting a little darker with each passing week.

We spent a bit of time with Tom. My attraction for him was gone, but I loved going to his house. We would talk and laugh. We even talked about me sometimes. Tom was great to me. I've never understood why he puts up with the way Mr. Grumpy Pants belittles him, but maybe he just appreciates the free training more than I did. We always had fun when we went to Tom's—amazing food and just relaxing conversations.

Mr. Grumpy Pants didn't show his bad mood swings in front of Tom. I got to know Lori and Bob through Tom as well, an amazing couple who came to my rescue much later. Grumpy worked at Bob's gym part time. I liked them both instantly. That seemed to bug Grumpy. He would say awful things about Lori, and I never understood as she seemed so nice. Then he would put Bob's business sense down, and I remember thinking *He has a hell of a lot more than you do, buddy.* Of course, I never dared say that to Mr. Grumpy Pants. I only nodded and agreed with him.

About the middle of June, Grumpy was really in a bad mood, and I just couldn't take it. I sent him a nasty e-mail. I was done. I knew his moods were killing me. I dreaded training with him and cooking him his damned breakfast. So I was done. I was much stronger back then, so I sent an e-mail that basically said,

> *Dear Jackass,*
>
> *Your moods are driving me nuts. I'm sick of being yelled at and I never want to hear "fuck you" again. I'm tired of paying for everything we do. Why don't you make breakfast sometimes instead of me always babying you? Quit being such an ass! If you can't make breakfast what about coffee? We've been together six months and you have never done that once. You have never even put a plate in the dishwasher!!!!*
>
> *Mac*

It was longer than that, and let me admit, I took a strip off him that I have never taken off anyone. I was finally at wit's end. I have to admit, I had a bit of coaxing from my family and friends to get rid of this guy. I remember feeling pretty good when I sent the e-mail.

Well, he was some mad at me. I learned then that you never ever confront him with anything. If you're at the shelter reading this, I know you can relate. He blew up and started texting, telling me right off. So via text, I told him we were finished! And I meant it. I didn't need that crap, whether the steroids caused it or not. In honesty, I was kind of relieved. My heart broke since I thought he was going to be my husband, and I was going to rescue him, but I had enough. He called, but I wouldn't answer the phone. My friends and brother invited me out to where I used to go to blues jam. I missed going and was pretty excited about getting my life back. Somehow, I hardly saw any of my friends for the past six months. I couldn't figure out why that had happened, so I blamed the fact that I had been training for the powerlifting meet. I was oblivious to the isolation that had been taking place in my life.

Grumpy (now Mr. Miserable) started phoning and texting while I was out with my friends. They encouraged me to just hit Delete as they had seen the emotional rollercoaster I had been on. I finally went outside and took one of his phone calls. I mean, I loved him and wanted the insanity to stop, but he still owned me. All his texts and calls were breaking me down. They learn if they put you down and make you feel bad, you will eventually start believing that you can't do any better than them and no one else would ever want you. During the call, he went on and on about how awful I was. My e-mail was pretty bad. I asked him if at any time during the six months he had been out of line. His answer was no; he had been great to me. He said he knew that no one had ever treated me as good as he had, and I would regret breaking up with him. (I learned later that psychological abusers use that stuff to melt you down.) I gave up. I hung up. I mean, how a relationship can continue with that attitude was beyond me. I was willing to admit I had made mistakes, but he wasn't. When I hung up, I assumed that would be the last I'd hear from him. I was happy but sad all at the same time. I went back inside the pub and had a drink. Shortly after, I went outside for a cigarette. From out of nowhere, he appeared. It scared me a little because I knew he was mad as hell. He took my arm and pulled me across the street to his truck. I had no choice but to go; he had my arm. He had such a strong grip that it left bruises. He literally dragged me across the street. I wanted to run back inside and get my friends and my brother but never got the chance. It all happened so fast and was so unexpected.

Once inside his truck, he went up one side of me and down the other. I never argued or stood up for myself. I just agreed with everything he said because he was mad as hornet. I knew that if I agreed to everything he was saying, I would get out in one piece. I told him I was an awful person, that I didn't deserve him. I told him I was lucky to know him. I did everything I could to settle him down, but it still went on for over an hour. I tried to explain that my brother would come looking for me, but he needed to yell and swear and freak out until he calmed down. I was so scared, I shook. Once again, he kept pushing my face into the window of his truck. All I could do was close my mind, find a dark safe place to hide deep inside myself. As I reflect back on how that felt, I remember seeing his face all snarled and cruel as he screamed at me. Words were coming out of his mouth, but I had found a way to leave the planet. I eventually called that place my fetal position. I learned to go there whenever I had to. It's kind of like playing dead while a grizzly is attacking you, I imagine. It really messes you up. You can escape even when you're trapped. It's like God gives you the ability to hide when there is no chance of running. I think perhaps you leave half of your brain there, and you start to shut down completely. That's when the fog starts. From the first time you go into fetal position, part of you stays there. Even when the craziness subsides, you walk around feeling numb, confused, and lost. Any hope of clear rational thoughts is gone forever. I swear I spent the next two years suspended in space with only thoughts of damage control.

Finally, he drove me to the door and let me go, but we were back together, and I was to meet him at my place in an hour. And the stupid little codependent did just that because she thought she couldn't live without him. It's amazing how they get into your head and mess up your thinking. Inside I was curled into a ball, hoping no one would notice me at all. I was mastering the mental fetal position and didn't even know it. Once you've been in a mental fetal position, you normally find an addiction to numb the pain. For some, it's alcohol or drugs or maybe even food. For me, it was weight lifting. The gym became my life. If I wasn't lifting, I was doing cardio, sometimes for hours on end. I had learned to make myself numb and to self-medicate. When I was training, I did visualizations of my muscles gaining power and thought of nothing else.

Much like drugs, fitness can be unhealthy. I didn't realize it at the time. You may start out being a healthy little fitness freak, but then you're bodybuilding, doing diets that can permanently damage your kidneys. Then perhaps you are lifting such heavy weights that you have accidents and get arthritis in your spine. If you really go full force into gym addiction, maybe you'll start kickboxing to numb your pain. Each sport you try becomes more and more life-threatening, much like pot to cocaine to heroine. I was self-medicating myself with a very unhealthy lifestyle. Everything about my life and body began to change from the moment I learned how to go into mental fetal position, but I never saw it. At that time in my life, my gal pals were wishing they could be so dedicated to the gym. That still makes me laugh. Have you ever seen a bodybuilder without her spray tan? It's not all that different from a skinny little crackhead, only our open sores are on the inside, not the outside. I'm not saying that all bodybuilders are self-medicating, but I would like them to ask themselves why they are risking their health.

On June 27, Mr. Miserable and I drove my truck to Cranbrook, British Columbia, for his strongman competition. I think it was our best weekend in the entire year. I wanted this for him so bad. I brought special food and just catered to his every whim. I loved doing that. He didn't make me; I actually loved doing it. He was happy all weekend. And I was happy. I was Codependent Superwoman! We spent the weekend with a man named Greg, a wonderful man whom I knew from the gym. He was so kind and sweet. He had been on steroids for years and, a month later, died from his steroid use. He was nothing like Mr. Miserable; he was always smiling and happy. I think it was then that I wondered if roid rage made my trainer miserable or if he was just born that way. I can honestly say, I have done many wonderful things and travelled the world, but the strongman weekend was one of the happiest times I ever had. I was so proud to be by Mr. Miserable's side. I just loved him more than I thought humanly possible. We laughed. I will never ever forget it.

It all changed when we got home. I won't bore you with the details as I'm sure you already get the gist. The emotional rollercoaster had begun, and it never really stopped. We'd have a good weekend and break up the next. All the fights were the same, his freaking-out followed by an e-mail from me. Then we would fight via text, and I would apologize for everything, and we would get back together. I had a miscarriage in there, and his daughter was pregnant—none of which he could handle. It was one disaster after another, and we were both burning out. Everything was my fault. Never once did he ever apologize for anything. He was perfect, and I was bad. It became my way of life. The chaos became normal. We were lost without it. I know now that his life had always been that way, but for happy, bubbly little me, it was a whole new ball game and way out of my league. My friends and family watched me retract into this insane woman who made her life all about damage control and keeping the peace. Followed by entirely too much fitness. They hated Mr. Miserable, and many of them made it very clear. I can still hear my dearest friend Bill saying "Get that goddamned bastard out of your life." A few walked out of my life because they thought I was stupid to stay with him. I was so wrapped up in the drama, I couldn't see the horse for the fence. Chaos was all I could relate too.

My best example is when a soldier comes back from war and has forgotten how to live. That was me. Somehow, living on the front lines was now a way of life.

CHAPTER 3

The chance to go to worlds was as gone as my baby.

My daughter Paige announced that she was getting married. I was upset because she was so young, but happy for her because I love her now husband Kale. It meant we wouldn't be going to worlds. I was so disappointed as my extra money had to go to the wedding. I was going to be paying both my and Mr. Miserable's way to worlds as his job often didn't even make ends meet. I tried helping him with tips and insisted he set up a legal company. But most of what I said fell on deaf ears. He hadn't even paid last year's taxes, and he was still paying write-off expenses with cash. He never heard a word I said. I have now learned that when you come from a chaotic background, it's all you know, and chaos is your comfort zone. The sad part is, it wasn't my background, and the chaos drove me crazy.

The week before the wedding, I had a nasty fall down some stairs I was training on, and they feared I had broken my neck. Unlike our miscarriage earlier that month, Mr. Miserable was really there for me this time. He went outside the hospital and promised God that if I was OK, he would protect me until I died. It meant the world to me. I just knew we were going to get him through his bad times and live happily ever after. Somehow, I was going to rescue him even if it killed me. He talked about his childhood with tears in his eyes every few days. I was more determined than ever to help him put his dreadful past behind him. The whole thing was strange. We'd be happy and fine, and out of the blue, he would get upset about his parents or his past. It's like he needed to have a bad day, so he created it. I couldn't see that back then, so I just hung on and tried to keep things sane. I failed, of course, and started to become just like him. My kids paid the worst because they had to live with me. I was up one minute, sending him love letters, hoping he'd be happy, then stomping around my house, pissed off at his moods and retarded faces, the next. I had my training though, and no fall down some stairs could take it away. Being at the gym, pushing my body to its limits, was the one place I could keep myself from thinking about him. It was slowly becoming my drug of choice to numb the great pain in my heart. I was a full-blown gym addict. I will always struggle with this as a result of those dark days.

The wedding was July 27, and it was amazing. The day before, Mr. Miserable helped me decorate all day. On the actual wedding, he took my son so I could tend to my daughter. The whole thing went off without a hitch. I was happy, and I think he was too. That night he cried in my arms and said he had never been part of a family like that. I really believed that the happiness was the life he wanted. He'd been talking about marriage since shortly after we met, and I believed him. I really thought he was going to be my husband one day, if only his stress level would lighten. I went to bed that night believing that the next wedding would be ours. Oh, I wasn't stupid. I knew it was going to be tough, but I kept telling myself that if I could just love him enough, he would be OK. Life was grand—for at least a day or two.

Mr. Miserable didn't make enough money, and some of his clients made him insane. The traffic made him insane; his friend Tom was always whining (or so he told me), and everything in his life sucked. His daughter was in trouble. It just never ended. Night after night, he was miserable. I would try to hold him and tell him to hang in there, but nothing ever changed. He talked about his parents more and more. He wanted to go back to Quebec and see them.

I couldn't really understand because, for the most part, he described his father as an abusive bastard who denied him everything a son needed and deserved as well as a drunk. Then he had this weird love-hate thing with his mom. He'd talk about her boyfriends and that she was a slut and that he didn't know who his father was for years. And that she too was a drunk, but yet he missed them and wanted to go home. So Little Ms. Codependent took some extra work so we could go to Quebec. I thought maybe if we could face some of this, we would be OK. And I sort of wanted to meet the Monsters that made the man of my dreams cry every week. Tom chipped in and paid two hundred of Mr. Miserable's flight, so we booked the trip to Montreal. It wasn't the world powerlifting meet I was hoping for, but I was excited just the same.

We counted down the days until August 18. He told me so many stories about all the things we would do. I was just overjoyed. He was even going to take me dancing. I missed dancing most of all as it's my very favorite thing to do. He teased me and joked with me that his mom spoke no English. I fell for all of it. I was really, really happy. I packed a ton of food for our red-eye flight to Montreal because I learned that if I kept him fed and rested, hopefully, all will go well. Somewhere about that time, keeping him out of a bad mood became my life's goal. I was convinced that if I just busted my butt and kept everything running smooth, we would be OK. Why I did that, I will never know. I must have lost my mind. My codependency kicked into full gear. My middle name became Damage Control. It was exhausting and so much work. I packed a huge cooler of food for our flight because I knew if he got hungry, he'd start screaming at the flight attendants. I was scared to be in the plane with him for such a long flight. I wasn't scared for me but for everyone else on the plane. Looking back now, I chuckle at that behavior. I should have been scared for me, but instead, I did everything humanly possible to keep things calm until we got off that plane and somewhere where he could take his frustrations out on me where no one else could see.

We spent the first couple days in the city of Montreal, and it was the third time Mr. Miserable was truly happy. I loved his mom and aunt. I couldn't believe all the things he had said. His mom was amazing. I fell in love with her as instantly as I did her son. She didn't appear to be a drunk to me. We had a couple drinks at his sister's place, and she was fine. It was weird. She could have just as easily been my own mom; she was so kind to me. I related to her a lot. She raised her son basically on her own just like I raise mine. I'm pretty sure she hates me now, but I know I will always like her.

We left her place to drive to rural Quebec to meet his dad and stepmom. We stopped on the way at a big gym in Montreal to work out. We often went to gyms when we were out and about as we both loved to train. I'll never know what made his happy mood disappear that day, but from the moment we walked into that gym, he turned into a Monster. I had learned by then that if he was upset, I should go into a mental fetal position. It's the one where I agree I'm dumb and know nothing and, most of all, keep my mouth shut. When he got really bad about thirty minutes into the workout, I went and showered and stayed in the changing room, crying for an hour. I stood in the shower in this strange new gym, talking right out loud to my dad and God or anyone that would listen. You know the people that live in the ceiling tiles are safe to know the pain in your heart.

When he came out to meet me at the car, he said he was stressed about seeing his dad. I thought OK; I get that with all he'd told me about this Monster I was going to see. I couldn't really understand why we had spent all this money to go see him if it would only upset him more.

The drive to Danville was awful. Mr. Miserable was in a hell of a mood, and at one point, I got out of our rented car in the middle of nowhere and considered hitchhiking back to Montreal and flying home. That was the first time insane thoughts crossed my mind, but it was the first of many to come. I didn't have my purse or a dime to my name, and there I was alone, standing on the side of a deserted highway in Eastern Quebec. I just knew I couldn't be screamed at and pushed around for one more second. I'm not sure if it was lucky or unlucky, but he drove back and ordered me into the car.

Mr. Miserable's dad was as delightful as his mother. I was simply shocked. He reminded me so much of my dad (my hero) that it brought tears to my eyes. We got there, and I witnessed his father really reach out to his son, but Mr. Miserable was colder than I had ever seen him. The next two days were a living hell. We fought in silence when we were in the presence of his father, but at night, when we went to bed, I wanted to die. I was trapped somewhere in Quebec with this miserable ass of a man and wasn't even sure what I did to deserve it. All I knew was, I hated every second of being by Mr. Miserable's side.

I tried holding him at night just to settle him down, but he would just push me away and tell me off. I was so confused as to why he treated me that way. I still e-mail jokes back and forth with his dad, and he's very awesome. His stepmom is really great too. They made me feel so welcome. I just couldn't understand Mr Miserable, but I never lived his past, so I tried to justify his crap!

Then we went to Quebec City and went dancing. Aside from him almost getting into a fist fight, we had fun. It was only one day, but I enjoyed it. I have to admit though, the trip was awful, and I was sure glad to be home. I tried to talk to him in a little bistro where we had lunch. His response was that I needed a spanking, and he took me back to our hotel to do just do that. I learned my lesson, and I gave up trying to tell him how I felt.

CHAPTER 4

He was beaten and bruised beyond recognition, and somehow,
it was my entire fault. I wasn't even there!

Then the insanity began. I started getting prank calls a day after we got home. I told Mr. Miserable, but he never said anything to concern me. Making a very long story short, his ex-girlfriend was calling me and hanging up. She had done this during several of Mr. Miserable's relationships. He had been getting texts from her during our entire relationship but failed to mention any of it to me. Even as it came out, he told one lie after another about how much contact he had with her. All his friends told me that she had been stalking and terrorizing him forever. That she was mental and just stupid. Not running on a full deck. He hated her guts and called her horrible names. I kind of believed him mostly because I wanted to believe him. And his friends backed him up. Then I remembered him telling me about a different girl. The one he dated before we met. Apparently, she too went insane during their relationship and actually tried to run him over at one point. In the beginning, I used to feel bad for him having all these crazy ex-girlfriends and a stupid ex-wife. But by the end of August, I started to see a pattern there. I knew he had the ability to make a girl pretty crazy. I had walked a mile in their shoes, so I understood. His crazy ex continued to stalk us both, and after some contact the police, I said I had enough to lay charges, but

I didn't do it. I felt bad for her. I understood her. When I dated Mr. Miserable, he owned Me. I was nothing without him. He taught me that and did it well. He'd say things like "If we break up, you will come back and beg for me. You can't live without me, and I can't live without you." It was a crazy time.

By September my friends were putting a ton of pressure on me to get rid of this guy. They saw how truly unhappy I was. He exploded one Thursday because he caught me smoking. I still have the scars to prove it. I won't bore you with the graphic details of a horror-filled incident in my little garage. I finally snapped. I sent my nastiest e-mail yet. I was done. Between his lies about his crazy ex and his constant temper tantrums for no reason, I was completely burnt out. I broke up with him. And I was actually pretty happy about it. The first week was tough as I had no personal trainer and was really lonely. I knew I had done the right thing, but my heart sure ached for him. See, by this point, I only knew chaos too, and a peaceful life left me lost and feeling empty inside.

I hired another trainer at a different gym near my home where I wouldn't have to see him because working out was the one place my mind would shut down and stop worrying about his well-being. I was disappointed about not being able to rescue him but knew I had to let it go. I started bodybuilding and loved the hard work it took. Mr. Miserable and I had an almost mother-son relationship, and I worried constantly about how he was doing. It was so unhealthy, but it just happened.

A week later, I got a text at two forty-five in the morning. "Baby, I'm on my way to the hospital. I have been beat up, I need you." I didn't even think twice; I ran to the hospital, terrified that my Mr. Miserable was hurt. I had taken a sleeping pill but didn't fear for my own safety. I just knew he needed me. I walked in, and Tom was there, surprised to see me as Mr. Miserable and I had broken up. When Mr. Miserable turned around and looked at me, my knees buckled. His face was beaten beyond recognition. I ran to him to hold him. He pushed me away and said, "You caused this. Are you happy now? Look at my face, you little bitch, this is what you do to me." I was stunned. I hadn't even seen him in a week. He had been texting nonstop all week, but I had seen that they were just telling me how horrible I was, so I had hit Delete.

He had gone to a bar with Tom earlier that night. The bar was in a really bad end of town. I was confused as to why he went there, but the bottom line was, he got into a terrible fight. Two big bouncers had taken him into the parking lot and pounded the hell out of him. His eye was closed, his face was all black, and his sinus cavity had ruptured. He needed stitches too. The mood toward me was foul in the emergency waiting room, but I kicked into caregiver mode anyway. I was waiting for some ice from a busy nurse when he started to get really mad. He was being a dick to the staff, and they didn't like it. I put my hands on his knees and told him to stop acting that way. I actually said, "If you need to vent that anger, do it on me, not them, or they will never help you." I was an idiot. They finally took him into his room and stitched him back together. I had a nice chat with Tom. Normally, when Mr. Miserable was in one of his moods, Tom would just walk away like he had that night. Tom encouraged me with the way I could handle him. I was an idiot and believed our love was so strong I could endure anything. Tom told me he had never seen Mr. Miserable as happy as he was as when he was with me. He told me no one could settle him down the way I did. Apparently, my damage-control act was pretty good. And for some insane reason, Little Ms. Codependent liked that.

It was 4:30 AM when we got into the dark parkade. I reached out to hold Mr. Miserable's hand and try to comfort him. He just snapped. He told me he would have never been at that bar if we hadn't broken up, and it was my entire fault. His words had nasty hooked thorns and an array of colorful language. I was destroyed; I was just trying to make him feel better. I walked to my truck in the dark, alone and scared. I was in a daze. How could I have let this happen to him? I asked myself over and over. I assumed that Mr. Miserable had gotten lippy at the bar and probably had it coming because he would get that way sometimes, especially if life was hard or, God forbid, he was hungry. But I was his rescuer, and because I broke up with him, he was beaten up. I hadn't been there to keep him safe, and now he was a mess. If you hear this crap long enough, you actually believe it, and that I did. The guilt was just too much. I know most of you don't understand that, but as you learn about codependency, it will make sense.

The next day, I called him, and he came to my house. I tried to nurse his wounds and settle him down. His anger went back to depression for days. I did everything I could to try and make this up to him. My friends were positive I had lost my mind, and I lost a few more friends as people started to give up on me. My life was isolating itself to a world that consisted of caring for my Mr. Miserable. I kept thinking *Just love him more, and he will be OK*. Things got worse, not better. My rescue attempt was failing so badly. I paid for his mother to come see him, hoping that would help. It too backfired in my face as she made a comment that Tom had a nice house and Mr. Miserable didn't (or so he said). He hated his mother for that comment. He was so angry. Nothing I could do was helping at all. He used to scare me so bad. His anger was getting even worse, and it was always a direct result of something I had done, so taking the brunt became my duty. His favorite thing to do was get a hold of my hair and push my face into something hard or rough. My stairs were his favorite place. Sometimes I had to hide the rug burn with three layers of makeup. I quickly learned that whatever had happened, it was my fault. I was bad, ugly, stupid, and mostly just useless.

My daughter Mandy was getting more and more fed up with my down-in-the-dumps mood that she was considering moving to her dad's. That woke me up. She was my life, and I wasn't ever going to lose her for Mr. Miserable. So I sent another e-mail telling him we were done. I lasted a whole month this time. I even started dating again. I was filling my time with anything I could to stop worrying about Mr. Miserable. I lost twenty pounds by running three hours a day. I loved my new trainer; she was great. She had also known Mr. Miserable's ex-girlfriend, the one who apparently tried to run him over. She told me he was a Monster to that girl, and she was terrified of him and hated his guts. I met my friend Kyle at that gym, and he was another pretty boy who recognized what I was going through because he knew Mr. Miserable's ex as well. It was pattern, and I was far from being the first. Mr. Miserable would text me for hours, telling me how horrible I was. A healthy person would have changed her phone number, but I didn't. It beat me down, and like before, I believed everything had been my fault. He would e-mail me constantly, saying I destroyed him. I know now he was destroyed long before we met but sure didn't recognize it at the time. Life was just insane, and I felt like

I was dying inside. All my dreams and plans of the perfect life with my Superman were just crushed, and somehow, it was all my fault. He still had never done anything wrong in his mind, so it seemed hopeless. I only had a couple friends left because most of mine had walked out; they couldn't bear to hear what was happening to my life for one more minute. I felt alone and that I was to blame, a failure. I had promised God I'd help this man. I hurt every second of every day. I mean physical pain, in my chest. I actually got sick from it. I was at my lowest of lows during our month apart. I worked my body until it would drop. I went on an insane bodybuilder's high-protein diet, and that made everything even worse. Eventually, I started peeing blood, nearly destroying my kidneys.

I went back to school to try and fill my time with anything but thoughts of him. I got certified as a personal trainer. Then I got certified as a nutritionist, then an elite trainer. Then I signed up for life-coach classes. I was learning to save everyone but myself. In and among all this mess, I started training clients at two different gyms. I loved that part as it feeds my codependency in a healthy way. I was exhausted and out of control, but I was on a mission to forget Mr. Miserable anyway I could. It was hard when days of text messages filled my cell phone. All nasty and cruel and very insane. I was sick and tired and not taking care of myself at all. And one day, on my drive home from an exam in a city three hours away, I snapped. I had to put a stop to the insanity. Keep in mind his ex was still texting me as well. It was like my mind said being with him felt better than being without. At least no one was texting, calling me names over and over. I wanted it all to just stop! Somehow they make a place so miserable when you are apart that you just take them back to get some peace. I know that sounds crazy because it is!

I drove back to Calgary and went to the gym. It was the first time I'd seen Mr. Miserable in about a month. He looked awful, so sad and full of heartache. He was really nice to me, which was new for him since the breakup a month earlier. He kept trying to spot me as I lifted. He told me I looked good (gotta admit, that shocked me). It was good to have him at my side. The pain in my chest stopped hurting. He was just as pretty as I remembered, but he was sad and broken, just like me. Somehow, I managed to convince myself that his crazy ex had brought him and me to this crazy place. Again, if you're told something long enough, you believe it. And this will shock you: I finally gave in and agreed we should be married. I think I agreed as I felt like I deserved to be punished because I was such an awful person. Only an abused victim could ever understand, but that's truly what I believed. That embarrasses me now, and no one knows that's why I ever agreed to be married in the first place. I had this big idea that if he had security, that someone loved him, he would be happy. And if he was happy, I was happy; it was like my job. He said he loved me and that he could forgive me for all I had done to him, and we were engaged October 11.

Looking back, I laugh about that. I was such a mess. I was a drama queen in the truest form. My life had changed, but I was determined that it was a change for the good. I started to really pay for everything and my sales were down. Mr. Miserable wanted to buy a farm in Saskatchewan and run away from all the negative people in our relationship. And our friends were fuming that we were back together yet again. It was like they could see how unhealthy we both were, but we couldn't. I never wanted to move to no-man's-land, but if it would make him happy, I would have done anything. I learned later about how abusers isolate you but never knew it at the time. He wasn't an abuser in my mind. He would grab my arm, pull my fair, push me around once in a while but never hurt me physically, so this was not an abusive relationship. I couldn't figure out why people kept trying to tell me otherwise. They just didn't understand the horrible life my precious Mr. Miserable had been through.

We decided we needed a vacation because life was so awful. He promised to pay me back before we even left the country, and I booked the trip. I was so excited and happy. I counted down the days until the romantic getaway with my new fiancé. I was fantasizing about love on the beach, peace, and happiness. I would e-mail him every few days, telling him how in love I was and how happy he made me.

It was strange he kept our engagement a secret. He didn't want to tell anyone because I didn't have a ring. Seemed a little nuts to me as I didn't need a ring that bad. The classic codependent didn't need anything other than their loved one's happiness. In my heart, I wanted this amazing man to be planning a wedding with me. I wanted him to buy me a ring. The cost could have been fifty bucks. I just wanted the happy wedding planning that every girl dreams of. Like we had gotten through the bad times and won the battle. I was willing to pay for all of it. Unfortunately for me, Mr. Miserable was just stressed-out and could only focus on us moving away. My friends and family went into panic mode, but I ignored them, thinking they were silly. I was engaged to Superman, and nothing could ever take that away. I was trying so hard to ignore his bad moods and just be happy. My training was going awesome. However, Mr. Miserable made me quit training with the girl I had been working with and go back to training with him. I was busy powerlifting my heart out. My goal was a Canadian record, and I was on a mission! I probably averaged two to three hours a day beating up my body. My little gym addiction was in full swing. It allowed me to live in denial that my life was a mess. For the most part, I trained on my own, managing everything I could to avoid training with Mr. Miserable. Mexico was right around the corner, and nothing and no one could make me unhappy—or so I thought.

CHAPTER 5

Sometimes the best-made plans are complete disasters!

We finally made it to November 18, the day we flew to Mexico. On day 1, we just explored our five-star resort and enjoyed the warm weather. We held hands on the beach, and I was in romantic bliss. Mr. Miserable hadn't managed to pay me for his share of the trip, and my sales was down, but I knew he'd pay me back; he was Superman after all. I put any negative thoughts on a shelf and just wanted to be at peace with my beautiful man. I was looking forward to dancing and being in each other's arms every night. I didn't have to cook or clean or train my clients; I was just going to rest and think about nothing. I was looking pretty good and, for the first time in a long time, wearing a bikini, which wasn't so bad. We swam in the ocean the first day. He held me; it was the greatest feeling in the world. I really believed we had the world by the tail. We laughed and splashed in the ocean and pool. I was like a little girl living in a fairy tale. There were no words to describe how happy I was after months of drama and chaos. Mr. Miserable was still pretty down, but I was learning to ignore it and just try and be happy, and that was just the first day.

The first night of our trip, he announced that we weren't engaged. My heart sank. I was numb. Could this really be happening? He had all these crazy ideas, like he wasn't a man unless he bought me a ring and paid for the wedding. However, he was more than willing to let me buy him a farm in Saskatchewan. I was confused and didn't understand. I thought we were planning a wedding. I bought bridal magazines and was fantasizing about a romantic intimate wedding. He couldn't tell his dad and his pals at the gym that we were engaged. The whole thing was just strange, and I was totally devastated. He was talking, but it was like he was speaking another language that I couldn't understand. I thought the drama between us was over, but in reality, it had just begun. I remember thinking I would die. I mean seriously die from the heartache. I silently cried myself to sleep, curled in a ball, wishing I was home with my kids. I had been to Mexico many times, but nothing was worse than being there with him. We even had to watch another couple get married on the beach. The pain was just too much. I think chaos mode was getting the best of me.

I woke up early and went to the gym, leaving him to sleep. I needed my fix more than ever, and in my mind, training for the nationals was like cocaine to a crackhead. I ran so hard, I almost passed out, which would have been a happier place than the place in my mind that hurt so bad. I did so many bicep curls my arms lost all feelings. Then I went for breakfast to avoid waking up the miserable jackass that slept in our hotel room. I couldn't put it off any longer as it was 11:00 AM, so I went back to our hotel room. I woke him when I opened the door too loudly by accident. I was in shit for that; then I was in shit for working out without him even though I agreed to go with him again later in the day, which I did. Then I was in shit because breakfast was over and he missed it, and he would now have to have lunch. I just stood in the hallway, apologizing, telling myself *Five more days, and I would be home.* I did my best to pretend to be happy, but life had been turned upside down. We seemed to be together, yet the engagement was off. Thinking back to that trip is surreal. It's all a haze of pain in my heart that makes tears run down my cheeks as I type this. A normal person, who has never lived within this, would think the physical abuse would have hurt me, but nothing wounded me more than the psychological abuse he tormented me with that trip.

I considered just cabbing it to another resort and leaving him (another one of my crazy ideas I'm glad I didn't do). I wanted to run away from him. He was a grumpy man, and nothing could make him happy. I was giving up, thinking he would never be happy for more than an hour at a time. Then I went back into it's my fault mode. I convinced myself he'd been happy before me, and I made him this way. I pretty much drank a bottle of red wine every night just to numb my pain. I pretended to be fine, but something in my heart died in Mexico. He went psycho on some noisy kids at the hotel, and it actually made me laugh. I was out of damage control mode and really didn't care what he did anymore. I went to the gym early every morning. I pissed him off every day, but I just kept going about my business of pretending to be on a happy holiday. He slept a lot, which allowed me some space to walk alone on the beach and take photos and cry. I cried and cried and cried. People would ask me if I was OK, and my answer was always yes. I met a few men on the beach who hit on me. It should have made me feel good, but instead, it made me feel sick. For the most part, I hated men, and even more, I hated myself. I'd been dumb to want to marry this miscrable man and believe we could be happy. I was still the one person that could bring out his worst. I thought a lot about swimming into the ocean and not coming back.

The sun was shining, but my world was bleak with no color at all. I didn't swim off because I was reminded of my amazing kids and how they depended on me. They haven't had much of a mother for several months, and I knew that had to change. Everything had to change. I remember wishing I could go to sleep and wake up a month from then. That may have been when I left the relationship. I'm not sure, but I know it changed who I was. He could yell, scream, and push me around, and I never even really noticed. I think by that trip, I learned to stay in fetal position twenty-four hours a day. It was like living outside my body. The wounds in my heart (which I now know are caused by psychological abuse) had just caused me to shut down completely. It was like I wasn't even there.

I learned later that people who have lived in chaos since childhood will often create chaos if things are going well because that is the only world they know. All of a sudden, Mexico made perfect sense. If we were happy, he would change it. It was like having anything positive in his life scared him so bad he would create something to make him miserable. Unfortunately, no one told me that at the time.

I came home and told my friends and family that we weren't getting married. I was dying inside as they all said yahoo! I was just crushed. I took more clients and trained harder at the gym. Mr. Miserable walked around, pretending nothing had changed. But it all changed for me. I really believe when your heart breaks into so many pieces, it just shuts down.

My journal entry on December 3:

Dec 3

Trained hard at the fort today. Gave me some stress relief. The other trainers were talking about Mr Miserable again though. Apparently his ex told them all that he was violent and a control freak. I'm so glad he never has to hear what she said. She must have been an awful person. He can be rather controlling as to who my friends are but I am trying to believe it's for my own good. He has taught me that my friends are pretty controlling. He was grumpy and angry again today. He's so stressed. Our relationship is hanging by a thread. Still trying to heal from Mexico. Under some money pressure as I have to pay for Mexico by myself by the looks of things. It's hard God. Why must I be the mother, the cook, the cleaner, the caregiver and the bread winner too?

(See that little codependent go!) It was a bizarre time in my life. Looking back, I can see that I was busy protecting Mr. Miserable and then protecting my kids, but never once did I go for help and find someone to protect me. I really needed help, but I blocked it out as I was the queen of codependency. I should have gone to counselling and got some help to see how unhealthy this man was, but instead, I just kept going to the gym and self-medicating.

I saw no future for us but wanted to get through the holidays. It was going to be my last-ditch attempt to show him the love I thought would end his depression. Where that hope came from, I don't know. I do know that when I start something, I finish it, and I still hadn't let go of the idea that I could rescue him like he had asked me to the year before. I wasn't very good at admitting defeat. I had tried sweetness and nastiness; I tried ignoring him, telling him off, holding him, and loving him, and nothing had worked, but for some reason, I just wasn't done—getting close though.

CHAPTER 6

And the walls came crumbling down.

It was December 5; Christmas was just around the corner. I was still numb from the Mexico trip and living in depression, but I kept working and training. My ex-husband was taking my children for Christmas. It was going to be the first time without them for the holidays. That didn't help my doom-and-gloom as he had never taken them the entire five years we had been divorced. My mother was upset because we wouldn't have my children for the holidays, and more and more, she hated Mr. Miserable. That being said, I couldn't very well tell my ex that they had to stay because I was an emotional mess and needed my kids. So I pulled up my socks and attempted to plan an awesome Christmas for Mr. Miserable and myself. I spent money I didn't have as my business was almost at a standstill, but any logical thoughts in my head had left the June before.

My mother had seen enough. I was sending her to stay with her sister for Christmas, and she was positive I was falling apart. She and I had never been apart, ever, for Christmas. After my father died, my mom and I became inseparable—until Mr. Miserable that is. I had all but stopped the nightly phone calls and Sunday dinners. Without my knowledge, she called Mr. Miserable and asked him to break up with me. She explained that he and I weren't good together and that if he loved me at all, he should walk away. Mr. Miserable lost control on her.

He yelled and screamed and called her a f—ing bitch. My poor mom was devastated. No one had ever talked to her that way. Why I couldn't see how horrible he was is just beyond me. I don't think I let myself come out of fetal position long enough to even see what was going on in the world around me. I needed help more than ever, but even when people around me tried, I just made excuses for my Mr. Miserable.

I booked a dogsled trip and a hotel in Banff for four days. It cost me a fortune, but I was determined to get through the holidays. I think in my mind, I knew Mr. Miserable and I would end soon and wanted one last chance of enjoying with him (no idea what I was enjoying, but it was just what I did). I knew it didn't happen often, and you may not understand that, but when we were happy, it was amazing. We'd call each other soul mates, and I think we both believed it. After working for years in Asia, I learned that some people believe God gives us one soul mate, and we come back to this earth over and over until we make things right with that person. Only that person can complete us. I believed Mr. Miserable was somehow my responsibility to fix. Some days I still believe that, but I'm thinking I'll have to come back and try harder in the next lifetime based on this past year. Abusers convince you that you cannot live, breathe, or sleep without them, but I never knew that. In truth, there were many days when I could barely exist with the constant drama unfolding in my dark little world. I was starting to sleep more, waking only because my precious son gave me reason to get out of bed.

Mr. Miserable came home December 5 in his usual mood. Life was tough for him. I had hurt him with my new whatever-goes attitude and all my e-mails. His job sucked and wasn't making any money. He was putting everyone down. He would say horrible things about Tom and his mom and the gang at Bob's gym. It was just negative times ten. He was on a waiting list for foot surgery, which I think scared him to death. Trainers can't afford to be injured, or we make no money. He was a wreck. I felt bad for him as always.

That night we went to bed. I lay there, listening to him complain about his horrible life. I listened, but I wasn't really there at all. I didn't hold him like I normally did. At times I'm sure I even rolled my eyes. I was so sick of hearing all the same crap over and over. Then he started in about our wedding. I didn't want to talk about it as he had ended everything in Mexico. He wasn't getting my attention at all. Inside I stopped fighting with him, and he could say anything, but I refused to react. Then he started on about how he couldn't tell his dad we might get married. I had heard the same crap a thousand times before and was emotionally dead to him.

I couldn't imagine why he couldn't tell his dad. When I left Quebec the year before, his dad said he hoped I could put up with his son because he thought I was the best thing for him. I was pretty sure his dad would be happy for us. I tried but just didn't understand. All his friends told me I was good for him. Nothing made sense anymore.

Mr. Miserable ranted for about ninety minutes before I finally started talking. He pushed and pushed and tried to get me to join in his fight, but for over an hour, I just sat there saying nothing, refusing to be dragged into yet another fight. I had learned months earlier that responding with how I really felt could get me badly hurt.

He finally went too far, which I believed was his plan. I told him I didn't care what he did about his dad. That we weren't engaged, and it didn't matter to me what he was going to do about it. I honestly admitted that I was only hanging on to get through the holidays anyway. Whenever I tried to talk to him, his first remark was always "Fuck you!" On a good day, it was "Fuck you, bitch." I actually never swore before I met Mr. Miserable, but on that fateful day of December 5, I stood up from my bed, looked down in the eye at that son of a bitch, and said, "Fuck you, Mr. Miserable!" It felt kind of good to say actually. For a few seconds anyway.

It caused a reaction I never expected. He went insane. He bolted from the bed, screaming at the top of his lungs. I retreated back into the bed. He started pounding his fists on the oak banister in my hallway. He was going crazy. I curled into fetal position and didn't look up. He screamed and yelled so the neighbors could hear, but I can't remember what he said. He wasn't getting a response out of me, so he came back into the bedroom. He punched the light switch to turn it on. The metal socket box went right through the wall. The drywall was all smashed, and the face plate was in pieces on my floor. Then he punched my wall again and again. He went for another light switch and put it through the wall too. Only this time, he cut his hand wide open on the metal box and sent blood all over the wall. He screamed, saying "Look what you do to me—you caused this! Get your ass out of bed and fix my hand right now, you bitch!" I was curled into the tightest ball I could make. He picked me up by my hair and threw me against the busted wall. I curled in a heap on the floor, fearing for my life. He used his foot to roll me over. Frozen in my mind, I knew I had to do what he said or perhaps he would kill me. It was honestly the first time I thought I might die. He was so big and so strong while I was useless. Knowing you have no power and someone can take your life is a realization a woman should never have to know. Men and women were put on this earth to protect and care for each other, not destroy each other. The mental anguish that takes place lying on the carpet in a ball will stay with you forever if you don't reach for help. I should have called the police, but that thought never even crossed my mind. By that time, I felt so useless that I wouldn't want to burden the cops when they had real people to look after. People who were important, and in my mind, that was not me.

I went and got my first aid kit and tried to stop the bleeding. I never spoke; there were no tears, just fear. He told me over and over "You do this to me. You make me this way." My hands shook so badly as I applied pressure and tried to get the bleeding to stop. The fear just took over my mind.

I bandaged his hand and went back to fetal position on my side of the bed where I lay until he went to sleep. Once he started snoring, I walked downstairs and stood in my kitchen. I just stood there. I had no thoughts, no feelings, nothing. I was just dead inside. I slept on the sofa, hoping I would wake up and it would all be a bad dream. I wished that not only that day was a dream but the whole last year had been a dream. I fantasized about having the life I knew before I had met him. Even being with a man that didn't need me or love me was better than this. I crept into bed before he woke up. I was scared that if he discovered I left the bed, I would be in trouble. I felt him stir and knew he was awake, but I didn't rush to make his breakfast in bed. I stayed tucked into a ball, afraid to move or say anything. He hadn't killed me physically, but mentally, I was as dead as a person could be.

Finally, he spoke. He asked what I wanted him to do. With my head hidden in the pillow, I told him I wanted him to leave. He got up, got dressed, and walked out my door. Then the tears began. I cried until noon, I think. I cried about my entire life. I was in shock and couldn't even function. My plan was to never ever see that Monster of a man again. I would sit on my bed and look at the holes in the wall and his blood splattered on the paint. I vomited four times, and my head throbbed terribly. I was physically and mentally finished.

My pal Ronnie called and wanted to take me for a drink. Vodka sounded like a really good idea, so I agreed to go. My Monster called and texted, but I just ignored my cell phone. When we fought, he would text sometimes thirty times an hour. He called my house phone, and without knowing it was him, I answered. He was being sweet and kind. He wanted to know what I was doing. I was numb, and nothing he said was even registering. I told him I was going to the blues jam with Ronnie, and he asked if he could join me. I remember telling him that it was a public place, and he could do whatever he wanted; I didn't care. Then he wanted to see me first and drive me to my blues jam. I said no, that I was going with Ronnie. She was one of the last friends I had left. We had made a pack that if I loved him, she would too. She's a codependent, just like me. Ronnie had a tough childhood and always felt bad for my Monster too.

When he couldn't drive me to the blues jam, he decided he needed to come to my house and change his clothes as he had been training a client. I said, "Do whatever what you want." My doorbell rang thirty minutes later. I didn't even answer it, so he just came in. I was in the kitchen, cleaning up. He came over to me and tried to hug me. I walked away, not wanting his touch. He took my hand and pulled me to the living room. I was confused as he was being really nice. He was still saying that I caused what happened with the wall, but he said I didn't deserve it. I think that was the closest I ever got to an apology for anything he ever did. Once we were in the living room, he fell down to the floor. I thought his foot was bad (the one he was waiting on surgery for), so I went down to the floor too and asked if he needed an ambulance or some stupid thing like that. He told me to get up. I was dazed and confused. Then he pulled a beautiful ring out of his pocket and proposed. I remember just standing there very confused. I looked deep into his eyes where I saw a frightened little boy who was putting his heart out there, and I couldn't bear to hurt him the way everyone always had. I stopped for a moment and, somehow, decided I had been such an awful person that I deserved a man like my Monster. It was like punishment from a god who surely must hate me. So I wrapped him in my arms, put his ring on, and made everything all better like only a good codependent can. I denied myself, my hurt, my fear, and my anger. I just wanted to help this broken little boy. Forget the hurt little girl in me; it was all about poor Superman! Right back into rescue mode I went. I now know I should have rescued myself, but I was too busy for that.

Chapter 7

*If life is like a box of chocolates, I must have been
giving them away.*

I was determined to have the best Christmas ever. I did all this family research about his family clan and wrote him a book. He was of Leviish decent, and his history was very fascinating. It gave me a place to leave the world behind. It was a romantic tale about two people based on him and me only set back in Celtic times of love and magic. I bought him some of his family tartan as he seemed to know nothing about where his people had come from. It was fun. Then I bought a ton of other things he needed. My Monster had been poor most of his life. He even lived out of his car for a while before we met. Instead of seeing that, at his age, it showed he had some problems and wasn't stable, it just made me feel bad for him, which really fed my codependency. My plan was to give him a gift every hour on Christmas day. We were planning to go to China together on my next buy, so there were many things he needed. I filled myself with shopping and training.

The dogsledding was awful; it was minus 21°C, and we froze. The dogs barked, making him nuts, and it was just not a trip I would recommend to anyone. We tried to thaw out at our hotel, but he was just miserable. We went to bed Christmas Eve fighting about his dad yet again. No sex, no romantic Christmas, just another of my Monster's bad moods. So much for the nightie I had bought to try and impress him. I had learned that my body would never impress him. The first six months I was fat (at 135 pounds), and he was going to get me in shape. Then in the fall when I lost all my weight, I was too slim, and my breasts were gone. He would never be happy with me, not sure why I tried. Once he was watching a video of a strongman competition, and I walked by the screen and he said, "Who's that fat ass?" I looked at him thinking *That fat ass is the one tending your every goddamned need, you idiot. That fat ass is the one that forgives you for everything and takes all the blame herself. That fat ass loves you no matter what you do. That fat ass has spent her last dime trying to rescue you. That fat ass bends over for crappy sex whenever you want it and asks for very little in return.* I wish now I had said it all out loud!

When I woke up on Christmas morning, I watched him sleep. Only this time, he wasn't beautiful at all. He was ugly. He had crooked teeth and a receding hairline. His muscles were built by steroids, not by blood, sweat, and tears. They no longer represented anything to me. He squatted a ton at the gym, so his body wasn't symmetrical; it was just ugly with this huge ass—eww, he was gross. His breath stunk, and he farted all the time. He was starting to really turn me off.

I gave him the gift every hour. It was dumb and made him feel bad. I had gone too far in my let's-rescue-my-Monster plan for both of us. He gave me a beautiful necklace that I cherish but never wear. We went to a nice restaurant for dinner, but as usual, he never had a compliment for my hair, my dress, anything. We never talked about me, just him and all his troubles. We redid the my-parents-suck conversation, which I can now quote word for word and even put the tears in my eyes as I recant it. By the end of dinner, he had himself in such a mood that was just angry about everything. I tried reading the book I had wrote him, but he needed chaos not love stories, so he was bored and didn't care to hear what happened next. It didn't even hurt me; I was so shut down by that point, I expected no less. I shut down my computer and quit reading after chapter 1. Never to this day has he ever asked to see the book I wrote him. I put hours upon hours into our story. I drank my usual bottle of wine at dinner in hopes of falling asleep fast and forgetting it was Christmas. I knew wine was not a sleep solution, but it was the only answer I could find at the time. He needed to bitch and complain about his dad for a while. He'd been telling me for weeks that he was going to tell his dad we were engaged on Christmas day. But when he finally called him, he never even mentioned it. I was pissed. I had hoped that once he told his dad, his dad would congratulate him, and we could stop crying about how his father never approved of anything he did. By not telling his dad, this conversation could go on for weeks. I was so sick of all the drama and chaos. I tried going to bed early, but he needed to still fight about his dad. I was mad that he hadn't told him, but for the most part, I was just silent. I couldn't bear to listen to his crap anymore.

I got up and started packing my suitcase. He wanted to know what I was doing. I told him I was going home. That he had wrecked my Christmas, and he sure as hell wasn't wrecking my Boxing Day too. I knew in saying this I might end up wearing my suitcase, but I didn't care. At that point, it would have been worth it. Anything other than listening to him whine and complain and put me down. He was mad as hell like usual. So he started packing his stuff too. We were out of the hotel in less than ten minutes. All my Christmas baking and the special meals I made ahead for us were shoved into the cooler, and we left.

We got back to my house, and he asked to come in. I didn't even answer him. I just went inside and locked my door. Christmas was a disaster, and I had nothing to say to him anymore. The next day, his usual texting charade began pretty early. He had left two new sweaters at the hotel, and of course, it was my fault. I was so used to everything being my fault that it hardly affected me. I knew I was a lousy girlfriend, too fat or too skinny, too stupid, talked too much or talked too little. I was living in a place where every move was the wrong one, and I was used to it.

My journal entry from December 25:

Dec 25

It's midnight and I'm home. Wicked fight with my Monster. I got frustrated because he said he'd tell his dad about the engagement and didn't. I was mad as hell. I try to understand his bizarre relationship with his father but I just don't. I wish I could talk to him about this but he gets mad and says such nasty things . . . I'm getting good at that too. What's happened to me. I'm swearing big time. Who am I? Does anything make this man of mine happy? Is it possible? Maybe he will never be happy. Maybe he will wake up every day for the rest of my life and say "fuck" All in all my worst Christmas yet! I miss my mom and vow to never spend another Christmas apart.

I decided I wanted out of the house. I had spent seven hundred dollars on the hotel and had three days left, so I drove myself back to Banff. I picked up Paige, my daughter, on the way, and we had a wonderful time. My Monster was pretty angry to hear I went back and proceeded to text me nonstop. For the most part, I just ignored him. I knew I would have to deal with him at some point, but for a couple days, I was just going to have fun. Paige and I went to a bar with live music that night and had a blast. Not sure where the ski bunnies were that night, but Paige and I were superpopular. The men lined up to say hi. It felt good. I was pretty, or so they said. I was funny, or so they said. In my mind, I was going to forget my Monster even just for one night. I didn't cheat on him and never would have. I was just doing something for myself for a change. Paige answered a few of the Monster's texts, but I didn't even care what was being said. I was running away and forgetting all of it. I laughed all night. We got home at like 3:00 AM, and I wanted to stay out even later. It felt like forever since I had laughed and felt good. I am pretty sure that Mr. Miserable was realizing he was losing me at that point.

Paige and I finished out the planned weekend in Banff by playing. It was awesome. We shopped and soaked in the hot tub (something I love and the Monster hates). I did talk to him a couple times, but for the most part, I pretended he didn't exist. I knew I'd have to deal with him when I got home but wasn't ready for that. We stopped in

Canmore on the way back to the city. Paige really wanted to go home as she missed her husband, but I was the opposite. I never wanted to go back again. I dragged her through every shop in Canmore, just putting off the inevitable.

Eventually, I returned, and as expected, my Monster was at my house within ten minutes of my homecoming. I had wanted to go see my friends at the blues jam, but he told me if I did, that we would be done. I apologized for how awful I'd been. He said I deserved a spanking. I cooked him dinner, and everything was fine. He went to bed, and so did I. We didn't even hug. It went pretty smooth actually, but I was still numb, and he couldn't have affected me if he wanted.

We met with his surgeon right after Christmas. That was the first time anyone gave me a card to the shelter. At the time, I thought those women were crazy. My Monster was stressed about meeting the doctor and how long he'd be off work and was in his usual foul mood. I stayed silent on the drive up just like I had learned to do so well. When we got to the doctor's, he was told he had to go for more X-rays. This sent him right over the edge. Sounds simple enough for most, but when you're as stressed as the Monster, the simplest of tasks can turn into a circus. He barked at the girls behind the desk and was being a complete monster. I knew it wasn't about the X-rays but about the stress he was feeling over the surgery. I sat him down and filled out his paperwork and put something wrong on the form. He was supermad at me and asked if I was dumb. I could see the nurses watching, so I knew I had to settle him down. I put my hands on his legs and quietly said, "Look, we need these people's help if we are going to get your foot fixed. If you have to be mad, do it to me later when we get home, so they don't kick us out." What an Idiot I was.

We waited in the X-ray room forever, and he was being ignored by everyone. I worried the doctor would leave before we got back, and then he'd really be mad. I left him in the x-ray room and went back up to the doctor's office to make sure he was going to be there for us. It was then that one of the nurses spoke to me about the shelter. She started out asking me what the Monster weighed. He was now roided to the max at 260. Then she asked what I weighed. I was down to 117. She told me no one was allowed to talk to me the way he did, and that it was abuse. I argued, saying "Oh no, never, he's just stressed about his foot. He's not abusive at all." She gave me the card to the shelter. I thought she was a silly old bird. My friends had been expressing concern for months, but the idea that I was going through abuse was insane. I wasn't being hit. I thought everyone had gone crazy.

CHAPTER 8

It's a mother's duty to put her children first . . . Thank God
I knew that much!

His surgery was scheduled for January 12. We were told if he didn't have it, his foot might be inoperable within six months. I had been planning to try and get out of the relationship, but how could I do that in his greatest hour of need? He would be off work for two months and unable to walk. And who would do damage control if he got miserable? I'd seen him in the doctor's office and couldn't imagine how bad a hospital stay was going to be. I felt like I was the only one who could help. Oh queen of codependency.

It was that day I made a vow to him. I promised to be there through the surgery and his recovery. That somehow I would pay his bills and nurse him back to health. I promised he could count on me. I told him several times, if he had to be angry to take it out on me. I could handle anything. I made a promise that I had no idea how I was going to keep. It's the one promise I regret more than anything in my life. As I reread that promise in my journal just now, I smacked myself in the forehead for being so bloody dumb!

The few days between Christmas and New Year's were tough. He was stressed to the max about his foot and how he would manage. He only had a few clients left and couldn't pay his bills. He asked to borrow six hundred from me. I was hurting financially, but of course, I gave it to him and some extra in case he needed anything.

We went to my friend Ronnie's for New Year's. Much like Christmas, it was a disaster. I'll let my journal entry sum it up for you:

Jan 01

Crap new year's sucked. The party was bad. Mr Miserable was stressed and spent most of it watching some blood and gut bullshit on T.V Mandy and my friends asked why he was being such a stick in the mud. I explained that he was just stressed about his daughter's baby coming. Heather said everyone has problems but they can be sociable. I wish I could teach him this, but just seems impossible. If we are with my friends he's not happy and that appears to be my plight in life. Now he's started putting Tom down. It breaks my heart. I loved how close they were. I judged his character on that when we first met. Starting to wonder who this guy is. I wish we could talk about this but he'd get mad and I so can't handle yet another fight. I need to be happy. Money is still struggling. Branden has me worried and I feel so alone.

So Christmas was a bust and so was New Year's. I didn't matter how hard I tried; the man of my dreams was a nightmare, determined to have a lousy time in whatever we did. My birthday was next. I'll leave that little disaster to my journal entry as well:

Jan 05

Yet another fight with Mr Miserable. My birthday seemed to be a big pain in the ass for him. He didn't have time to get a gift and I bought the dinner. It wasn't a money thing at all. I feel hurt. I feel like I bust my ass to make his life special and I deserved this one day to be the one treated well. Why can't I be taken care off . . . on a total pity party today. I lost Dan to Cali last year on my birthday and this one was no better. I hate my birthday. Miserables ex texted him again. Why me God? I could just give up. Will every holiday suck? Does my Monster like to be miserable? How can I change this before I go crazy. I wish sometimes we could just talk and not fight all the time. I have started saying Fuck you back to him and I am ashamed. I know how much it hurts to hear it, but yet I say it. My goal right now is to find the strength to get him through this operation. I'm worried he's going to be grumpy and my kids will notice. I pray for peace and strength.

Wasn't real thrilled with the way 2009 was unfolding, but the plan was to just get him through this surgery, then maybe he would settle down. I kept my needs on the shelf like the perfect codependent always does.

His ex, who had been texting and calling for months, finally got the best of me. So I called her. It was interesting. She sounded pretty nice. She told me how he treated her, which was no big surprise to me. She told me he left her in debt and feeling used. Then he'd come back for sex whenever he wanted. He'd reel her in and then throw her aside. I understood why she was so nuts. If I'd been doing that for five years, I'd be a bit off the wall myself. Hell, I'd been doing it for a year, and I was starting to snap. I asked myself if I would be just like her. The call with her was a good thing. For a brief moment, I knew I wasn't alone. I know that sounds crazy, but it was how I felt. I think it may have been at that moment when I started to question everything being all my fault. And the fact that I brought out his worst.

My Paige was concerned about my well-being and had a surprise birthday party for me at my blues jam place. Her intentions were good, but like everything else, it was a disaster. The party started out fun. So many people came. Some of my Monster's friends, like Bob and Lori, came and Tom. It was really amazing how many people showed up. I had been isolated for so long and really didn't expect half of them to be there. It got to the point where I couldn't get a text message. I didn't have to explain to the Monster, and no phones were allowed to be answered, even when it was my mom. It was insane as I had never cheated on him. He hated all my friends and picked them apart every chance he got. I actually started to believe some of the things he was saying. I almost looked forward to moving away. My happy social-butterfly days were over. By my birthday, I was only allowed to answer the phone calls he allowed. Every single text message I received was always read by him. He knew my every move. He never left my side even when I went to the bathroom.

Toward the end of the party, my brother got drunk and embarrassed me, and then his girlfriend showed up. She's a drunk and a bad one at that. The moment I saw her, I knew the gong show would begin. She started in on me, and the next thing I knew, she pushed me. She's always been really unstable. I know now that my brother is a codependent just like me, or she would gone. It's weird I could see it in them but never in myself. When she shoved me, I pushed her away, and my Monster caught her by the throat and pinned her down, holding her by the throat very firmly. My Monster held her there for a while, and she couldn't breathe. When she came up gasping, she was terrified, with tears in her eyes and her face all blue. He could have killed her, but I knew he never would. It all happened so fast but pretty much put the party to an end when the bouncer threw my brother's girlfriend out of the bar like he had so many times before.

That day pretty much finished any friendships I had left. Of course, I defended my Monster because it's what I always did. I'm not a fan at all of my crazy sister-in-law, so I have to admit having someone stick for me was pretty awesome too. But his temper did go way too far. My Paige vowed that as long as he was in my life, I would never see her or my granddaughter and son-in-law again. My pal Heather got mad at me, saying I was next and for me to get out. My brother said, "He'll beat you soon." My mom panicked and got all worried. My ex-husband even called me to see if my Monster was abusive. But my answer was the same to all of them. He was stressed-out and would never hurt anyone. I wish I could have been honest and told just one of them what was going on, but I just couldn't betray my Monster like that.

I was so embarrassed in front of Bob and Lori, I wanted to die. I kept thinking *Why me?* I was a happy-go-lucky girl. Why was drama following me everywhere? I was living in hell and getting more alone by the minute. I quit talking to my friends and telling them anything that I was doing as they all hated my Monster enough already. And he hated them. I felt so bad for my Monster; he just never got a break.

My good old Ronnie stood by me though. She always turned a blind eye and let me make my own choices even if she knew how stupid I was. It was the best thing she ever did for me. Oh, she expressed her opinion and was terribly worried, but she loved me through it all. I will be thankful for her until the day I die. She was the best friend I had.

We got through the day of the surgery far better than I expected. He wasn't miserable at all. He was thankful to everyone and was really great. I was so relieved. I did, however, stop by the nurses' station on my home that night and explained that he could be edgy sometimes, and if they needed me, I could settle him down; just call, day or night. Oh, they called all right, at six thirty the next morning. They were ready to call security and have him restrained. He wanted a bath, and no one had time, so they gave him a pack of wet ones. He just blew. The nurse on the phone asked me to come fast. I flew to the hospital because I knew they didn't understand my Monster at all. The nurse referred to him as abusive, and I was presented with yet another business card to get some help. I wondered why so many kept saying that when he was just stressed-out.

I got to his room to find him pretty upset. I bathed him like I had the night before and told him if he needed to get mad, to get mad at me because the nurses wouldn't understand. I can't believe I actually suggested something so stupid yet again, but I was actually that insane. Like I said, attack me. I can handle it; they can't. I roll my eyes now just thinking about the craziness of it all. I'd raise my little hand and said, "Pick me when you're mad!" And now I'm supposed to tell you he abused me. I'm thinking I requested a good part of it due to my codependency. Don't get me wrong; no one has the right to treat a person the way he did me, but I know I played a part in it. I allowed it without getting help; it was all I knew.

He did pretty good the next day, but I got sick. I caught strep throat and a double ear infection while I was in the hospital. I should never have tended to my Monster; instead, I should have been home in my bed, but a team of wild horses or a 104-degree temperature wasn't keeping me from caring for my Monster as I had made a promise, and I keep my promises. I may have been a crumby girlfriend that drove him to a terrible temper, but I was a girl of my word.

The nurses called again on his last day in hospital; he wanted to go home, and they couldn't do the paperwork fast enough. All hell was breaking lose. When I arrived in haste at their request (still very sick), the nurse was crying, and some old bat was about ready to go punch him. I said, "Come on now, ladies, it can't be so bad. I can handle him." I walked in the room. He was trying to dress and had all the tape off his IV. He was cursing away about how incompetent the staff had been. I tried to hug him and just get him to take some deep breaths, but he was pissed off. He shoved me into the wall, causing his food tray to go flying and my head to hit the floor yet again. I was getting pretty good at picking myself up and putting a smile on my face. I knew it was going to be a fetal position day for sure. My journal entry that night reads,

Jan 14

Brought the Monster home. He's really grouchy. I am super sick. I shouldn't have been driving but couldn't leave him there. My kidneys are bad too. He was some mad about my bad driving. I feel like no matter what I do it will be wrong. Please God make the kids behave so they don't upset him more. Heal him fast . . . I'm exhausted. Send someone to help me. I want to go to bed and get well, but there is no time. Stressed about money . . . the cheques to my Monster went through . . . Send me some work God, but heal me first and of course my Monster.

Two days later, there was no improvement.

Jan 16

One hell of a day again. My Monster is mad at the world or just me not sure which. It must be hard for him as he isn't used to being cooped up. I wish there was no T.V in my room as I need sleep so bad and he stays awake and turns it up when I cough. I can't help the coughing but find myself apologizing all the time. The kids are frustrated with having to be quiet all the time. This is hard. I tried to talk to him so maybe we could solve some of this but he doesn't want to talk and basically told me to get out of my room and leave him alone so that's what I did. I really wanted to go to bed and get some sleep so I could get well. Is this how my life will be forever? Going up to try and get him to play a board game and maybe just maybe cheer him up.

Well, Monopoly worked for a few hours, but as soon as the game ended, he went right back to his mood from hell. My kids retreated to bed even though it was still early. I curled up in a ball, hoping my antibiotics would kick in so I could get well and care for my Monster. I just needed sleep. I was physically and mentally exhausted. I prayed that I wouldn't cough because it ticked him off so bad. Then he wanted a bath. So I got up in the middle of the night and helped him into the tub. He was not doing well at all. After yelling at the nurse at the hospital, she panicked and gave him sixty narcotic painkillers instead of six, so he was in rare form. Wacked out on OxyContin, stressed-out on pain meds, withdrawing from a week of no roids, and most of all, hating me. He hated everything I did or said. It was bad. He had gone to the bathroom before we set him into the tub and left a bit of poop all over edge of the tub. He was mad about that, and I tried to clean it as fast as I could, but I couldn't even clean his crap good enough. I was bent over the edge of the tub, trying to wipe it up, and he pushed my face in it. He rubbed me hard into the cold porcelain, telling me I made him feel like shit. I was positive my nose broke, and his shit stained both my cheeks. That's probably when I just wanted to quit living the most: the night of the shit on the bathtub. I laugh now, but was crying at the time.

He'd had enough of my shaking and walking on eggshells and told me that if I didn't change my attitude, he'd go home. He acted like it was some gift to me that he was in my home. I was so sick that caring for him was the last thing I was up for. As I heard the words escape his lips, I finally reacted. In my mind, I was thinking *You ungrateful bastard.* I asked if he felt ready to go home. He said no, but he didn't have to put up with me and would if I didn't smarten up. Much to his surprise—and mine too—I started packing his suitcase and hauling stuff to his truck. Then I got him out of the tub and dressed him. He was so mad. He should never have been driving, but I have to admit as his trucked backed out of my driveway, I was relieved. My journal entry from the next day reads,

Jan 18

> *Still feeling broken but doing better. I am dealing with the guilt that my Monster is at home and he has no money when I promised to help him. I know if someone was going to pay my bills and take care of me I'd be kissing there ass not telling them off. Just got a letter from my Monster where he tells me how great he is and how screwed up I am. Like all his other*

girlfriends I guess he knows how to pickem. Got told Fuck you hopefully for the last time. He went on about dad again. Talking about how my dad spoiled me rotten and ruined me. If only he knew what a jerk my dear old dad could be. Dad could be such an ass when he wanted but I have chosen to remember the good times and not the bad. How I wish my Monster could learn to do that. Being happy is a choice not a privilege. Today is hard but I will choose to be happy and put on a smile as I am head of my family and they need me. I will return all of Monsters stuff today . . . so not looking forward to that. Gathering it all up just sucked but I am strong and I did it. Not even a tear although my heart is crushed again. I know I will always love him, but I also know I can't help him, he has to do that and I don't think he wants to. I have learned that rather than being grateful for the amazing life he has, he chooses to be angry for what he doesn't have. I believe he wants to be happy and loving, but doesn't know how. I used to think that was teachable, but now I realize it is a gift from God and for that I am grateful. Today my prayers are for my Monster. God heal him fast. Send him money for food and rent. Send him a girl that understands him and is stronger than me or more understanding . . . maybe more patient and kind. I pray that you give him his farm and the peaceful life he longs for. I also pray that you give him a love for himself and the girl you send him. Don't let him wallow in self pity show him how lucky he is. Show him how great his life is so he can stop being so stressed and grumpy and go attain his goals. He's a good man and his smile will be sadly missed. Teach him God, he deserves it and so do his kids, his amazing friends and his mother who loves him so much. And please God don't let me see him when I dropped his things at his door.

Finally, the codependent was starting to give up. But that takes time, and believe it or not, I wasn't there yet. He was back in my house two days later, repeating exactly the same crap as the week before. I was feeling better as my meds had kicked in, but unfortunately, his were having the opposite effect.

I started training on weekends with a bunch of powerlifters at a new gym. They were all great friends of my Monster (or so I thought) and so helpful to me. The weekends and looking ahead to that powerlifting kept me going as the next few weeks unfolded. My gym time had always been my space where I left the world behind. Not to mention the kind people who seemed to accept me when I was falling apart. I never told them what was going on because I lost my other friends doing that. They seemed to really like my Monster, and that was sure a nice change over my family and friends. He was still grumpy as hell, but I kept telling myself *Four more days till Saturday's training. You can do it girl. You are strong.* I was training for nationals and hoping to break some Canadian records.

Later in the month, my best friend Ronnie had a birthday party for her brother at a place I just loved to go dancing at. I loved her brother like my own and was so excited to be getting out. Life at home had been in silence for the most part. I cooked and cleaned and let some clients go so I could tend to my Monster. He was miserable because he couldn't work out, and I felt so bad for him. I knew to stay quiet and tried not to set him off. He was screening every phone call and text I got. Sometimes he would tell me not to answer, and I did as I was told not wanting the fight. Inside I was hating him by the minute. He was getting uglier to me every day. I think we had sex once in two weeks, and it sucked. He was in a cast, so I was surprised that we managed it. But yet again, I did it because it was better than being hurt.

I begged to attend the party, but he said no. I explained to Ronnie that I wasn't allowed to go because my Monster's foot was hurting all the time. She was upset, and she was the last person I ever wanted to hurt; she had always been there for me. So I got brave and told my Monster he could stay home. That I understood but that I was going even just for an hour. Big mistake. He tried telling me no, but I insisted. So in the end, after a few good shoves, he decided to come with me.

He was yelling at me before we even arrived at the pub. Then we saw my friend Kyle at the door. Kyle hated my Monster and purposely gave me a hug and kiss, thinking he was helping. Kyle loved to get him going. That set him off more even though I hadn't seen that guy in months. He sat at the party being a complete jerk, pouting and acting like I dragged him there. It was awful, and I was embarrassed, wishing I had stayed home. I regretted going the moment we left. I wondered what happened to the girl that used to have such fun at those events. I wondered when the last time I had smiled was. I was as miserable as my fiancé, but I saw no cure.

The morning after the party, we had yet another fight. I told him his lack of effort at the party had let me down, and he just said "Fuck you" like he always did. My children went to their rooms every time my Monster got out of bed. I remember making chilli to try and cheer him up. I tried to cuddle with him, but he just pushed me away. I ran him another bath, hoping that would help. I watched as my kids did their best to stay out of sight, and that broke my heart. We had been together a year (which we never even celebrated), and my life had gone from pink to black. Life just sucked. Ironically, the Super Bowl was on that day, but I hardly even watched it. My Monster wasn't interested in football, so I didn't even ask for the game to be on.

I tried to talk to him while he was having his bath and see if we could get some counselling. He had said before Christmas that he would consider it. He wanted no part of it now. He said the only problems we had was me. That I turned my kids against him and made him the way he was. It wasn't true at all. My son wanted him for a stepdad. He looked up to my Monster and all his big muscles in the beginning. Or so I thought. Mandy hated him, and for good reason. He said I was the one with problems. I was the drama queen. I needed mental help. I have to admit, I was starting to realize I did need some help. I just didn't know where to go for that. I had a collection of abuse hotline business cards in my purse, but I still believed this wasn't abuse. My Monster was just a victim of his past, and I was just fine with his bad moods. In reality, I was as sick and screwed up as he was. He used to call us a team, and I wanted to be a team so bad, I bought him the sweatshirt! Oh, we were team, all right, one as sick and unstable as the other. I laugh now thinking at least we weren't wrecking two homes.

He got sick of my begging him to go for help after about ten minutes in the bathtub and told me to pack his things so he could go home. I calmly did just that. There was no fight; he just left, and I was glad to see him walk out that door. That glad feeling never lasted for long. I was like a fish on a line. He'd reel me and then cast me out, and I did exactly the same thing to him.

I was called to the school to meet Mandy's school counselor the very next day. Mandy had talked to her counselor about what was going on. Sometimes I think she was smarter than me. The counselor tried to advise me to get this man out of my life as it wasn't healthy for my kids. I didn't want to hear any of it. So she suggested that my Monster not be allowed in the home when my children were there. I completely agreed to that. When I called my Monster and told him what she had said, he agreed too. We could both see what all our drama was doing to them. Of course, it was all my fault, but he understood.

The next morning, we were supposed to go to the hospital and get his staples out. I had promised to be there, and he said he wanted me there. He agreed to pick me up at eight thirty. Our appointment was an hour later. I texted him at eight forty-five to see where he was as I had taken my kids to school early to pull this off, but he never answered. Then at 9:05, I texted again. His response was "Fuck, I'm on my way." I knew he was in his typical bad mood before he even arrived. I sat on my front step, waiting for him. He pulled up, so we got in my truck. He wanted to drive, and even though he was in a cast, I let him because he always complained about my driving. I went too slow or too fast; it was just never good enough. I always hated driving even since I was a child, but my Monster made it way worse. To this day, if someone is riding with me, I ask them to drive because I'm afraid I will screw up. I got in the truck and sat in silence. He said hello, so did I. Then it was silence, except for him telling other drivers on the freeway what bad drivers they were. He did this a lot. It kind of makes me laugh now. We arrived at the hospital but couldn't find a parking spot. I offered to park the truck and drop him off. At first he said forget it. But we were late, and after going around in circles and getting madder and madder, he finally got out and let me go park. I ran to the door to catch up, but he sighed, all ticked because I took so long. The waiting room was packed, so he sat down, and I went and got a number. He had some pretty sharp comments for me, but I was silent. I wondered why I was there. I felt like I made things worse, not better. After listening to him being a jackass, I finally said out loud, "So, Mac, how was your night?" Then I answered myself, "It was good. I slept well." This continued for a moment, and finally, my Monster said, "What the hell's wrong with you?"

"Just having some light conversation. Don't mind me." I think I was losing my mind. The tension was just so thick sitting next to him that I had to do something. They finally called us in. The nurse was Mr. Chatty Cathy, and my Monster was pretty cold to him. He kept looking at me in bewilderment. It was very clear that something was terribly wrong. As they started taking his staples out, he winced in pain. I threw all the bad feelings out the window and went to stand beside him and try to hold his hand. When my Monster was in pain, I would forget everything to go help. Somehow, him having surgery was my fault. I had encouraged him to do it. He shoved me away yet again and said, "What the fuck do you want?" I sat back down, feeling so rejected and hurt. That happened a lot actually. I looked at him and knew that was the last time he'd ever do that to me. As the pain got worse, he reached out his hand for me. I wished I'd pushed it away, but I took it. Being there was awful, and I hated it. The nurse asked if I was OK on the way out, and of course, I said yes.

I went and got the truck for my Monster so he didn't have to walk with his crutches. It meant I had to drive us home. He was really sharp and cold, commenting on how terrible my driving was. He told me that he just wanted to go to my place and get some sleep. I lied to him the first time ever. Typically, on a Tuesday, Mandy would go to her dad's along with her brother, but I told my Monster that she wasn't going that night and would be staying with me. So he wouldn't be able to spend the night. I had honestly never lied to him before that day.

He was upset, saying he had no groceries at home. I had lent him another $550, but he hadn't been able to go get food. I offered to take him for groceries and get them into his truck. I went to a store near my home, but it wasn't the store he normally went to. He preferred Safeway, and I was at Sobeys. Stupid mistake on my part. Then I parked a fair way from the door, thinking I would just go buy what he needed. He said, "Fuck, could you park any farther away?" I apologized and didn't realize he was going in. He got out of my truck and slammed the door. I walked slowly behind him in silence, a place I had come to know well.

First he wanted oranges. So we went to the produce section. He asked me which oranges were seedless. I was scared to answer, but I honestly didn't know. I looked at him for a moment in fear that my lack of an answer would set him off, and then I told him I'm not sure. He threw his crutches onto the floor with a crash and hopped up to the oranges. He told me I was stupid for my age to not know. I tried explaining that I was diabetic and hardly ever bought them as I can't eat them. He said I should know as I had kids. He put some oranges into a bag and threw them into my cart with a bang.

Then he wanted extralean ground beef. I was shaking from the oranges ordeal but seeing that there was no extra lean sent me right over the edge. He was mad as hell. He threw the crutches again. He wanted to know why I brought him to this stupid store when I knew he hated it. I didn't know he hated Sobeys, but I did know when he was home, he went to Safeway. Then he found extralean ground chuck and asked me what it was. Scared again, I said I didn't know. He said "Fuck" and threw a package of it at me. I had picked up his crutches again and handed them to him. I walked slowly behind him, pushing the cart. When he stopped, so did I. We just stood there for a minute, and finally, he told me to get up there. His foot was hurting, and he needed me to go get him brown beans, milk, and garbage bags. He planned to meet me at the till. I scurried off in a rush as I didn't want to make him wait. First the brown beans. I knew he normally bought the generic ones, but today the good ones were on sale and only two cents more, so I grabbed two cans of Libby's beans. Then I found the milk and hurried for the garbage bags. My heart sank. I had been in trouble once before because I bought black garbage bags, and he buys orange garbage bags. He claims they were better. At my store, the only orange ones were in a huge box, and they were around eighteen dollars. I was scared this might upset him, but I assumed I'd be paying, so I hoped all would be OK.

He was waiting near the till like he said he would be. His foot was killing him, and his crutches were causing problems too. He took one look at the cart, and loud enough for everyone to hear, he said, "Fuck, I can't afford a big box of garbage bags like that, and you know it. And I can't afford those beans." He was really mad at me as I had screwed up yet again. I said I thought I was paying, so it was OK. Then louder, he said, "No, I can pay for my fucking groceries. I want a bag of five orange garbage bags, and no more, and get the right beans this time." Everyone at the tills was staring. I was shaking like a leaf. I bolted for the generic beans. Got that fixed, but then I went to the garbage bags. Oh crap, they had no bags of orange garbage bags, only black ones. There I was in the middle of Sobeys, and I started to cry and cry. I was trying to pull myself together, but I was screwed. I grabbed a bag of five black ones and headed for my Monster. I frantically explained about the bags. He just said, "Whatever. Don't bring me here again."

It was about noon when we reached my house, and I parked in the driveway and asked for his truck keys so I could put the groceries inside for him. He asked why I was doing that. He said, "Aren't I coming in to your house? Mandy isn't home until four." I never made eye contact with him. I simply said, "Nope." I loaded his groceries and left him standing there. I went into my house, locked the door, slid down the wall into fetal position, and cried like a little girl. That was the last day my Monster and I were together as anything more than sworn enemies. It started at a coffee shop and ended at a grocery store in the same parking lot. The strangest thoughts go through your head when you are in that state of mind.

Later I went back to that store to get some groceries of my own. An older lady that worked at the till came up and asked if my Monster was my husband. I was embarrassed that she remembered me. I told her, no, he wasn't. She said, "Thank God! The way he talked to you today was abuse. You're a pretty girl. I always see you smiling when you're in here. Promise me you will get some help."

I explained that he just had his staples out and was in pain. She didn't care and just went on about abuse. I thought she was as nuts as everyone else who had tried to tell me.

CHAPTER 9

Love hurts.

I kept quiet for the next two days. I walked around my house in a daze. I was broke, borrowing money from my line of credit to pay his bills and mine. There wasn't going to be a wedding. The life I dreamed of was over. I asked myself if it ever had started. I thought about December when he proposed, and I had told him then that talk was cheap. He always promised that when he was less stressed, he was going to be good to me and the kids, but the stress never stopped. Oh, once he ran me a bath and lit candles all over when I came from school late. And three times he bought me breakfast at a place we both loved. And once he made me a CD with some amazing love songs on it. My birthday card was really beautiful, and the carnations he gave me after China were awesome. He trained me, but rarely was it fun. Everything else was usually him in a bad mood or him in tears or him stressed-out. I used to hate how he talked to his daughter. I prayed no one would ever say those things to my kids. I spent one whole night thinking about the broken promises.

He sent a couple e-mails. Here's a cut-and-paste of the first one:

> I just read the Christmas card you sent me where you
> said you'd love me forever what a farce!

I finally sent him this e-mail back:

I told myself I would never try to speak with you through e-mail as it always went all wrong in the past, but as we can't even speak I feel I have no choice. I never made you have this surgery. I believed it would help. My understanding was it caused you great pain and would be inoperable at some point. I offered to stand by as you went through it, but unfortunately had no idea things would get this bad. I also didn't realize at the time that I wouldn't be able to afford to support you financially. You promised me love and respect in lue of romance and the little things girls need (like the odd date) which hurt, but I don't feel you have been respectable or loving through this. Instead of appreciating all I was attempting to do for you and willing to give up for you, you focus on every little thing I do wrong. I am scared to speak for saying something wrong . . . it's so painful.

I think I did my best considering everything that has happened. I will always believe I was good to you and that I tried harder then you did to save the relationship.

I can't walk on eggshells around you anymore. God forbid I won't know good oranges from bad. I stopped and asked myself what I was getting out of this relationship. The truth . . . I'm not getting the things I need. I sort of saw my future of having a fiancé who was my friend. Someone to laugh with once in a while. Someone who would surprise me and do things for me (yes I am still labouring on about my birthday and our one year anniversary) I really planned on having someone in my life who when I cared for him he was happy. I mean not jumping up and down happy but grateful I did all I was doing and be nice to me. I feel I tried to be the best fiancé I knew how to be, but somehow it just wasn't returned to me. I have been accused of walking away all the time, but in my defence that has come from you making promises that you don't keep. I think your self-centred and incapable of thinking of anyone but yourself, I have sacrificed a ton here (Voluntarily) and you complain that you have to drive to my house and live out of a suitcase? At Christmas you said I did too much and it drove you crazy. I learned in that we are very different people. No one being better than the other, but not probably meant for each other.

I feel I have spent the last year being loving, kind, giving, and patient as you have fallen from one stress to another. I'm sorry but I'm just not getting enough back to keep trying or to hang on to hope that it's going to change. I fear I will always be waiting. Like I tried to explain on Sunday when you mocked me . . . my heart has slowly been dyeing. I used to get excited that you were coming home, and now I shake inside wondering what I will do to set you off this time. I used to look at you and be so attracted, but now I can't even look at you. I know I will be in shit for something or say something that will be laughed at or get a retard face. I have found it best to just be silent and hope I don't screw up. I can't live this way, and can't be excited about a future like this.

You have an opportunity to make some money from home, and sorry to be so blunt, but it looks like you haven't gotten off your ass and done it. I can't pay your rent next month I'm sorry but as you know I have had a huge business downslide. If I had it I would give it to you, but I don't.

I have tried so many times to talk to you about this but it usually just causes a fight that is somehow all my doing and as result we solve nothing. I'm scared to even approach you about the problems I think we have or worse yet my needs. So that being said all I can say is this is not good for either of us.

I'm sorry I have been such a letdown for you. All I can say was I did my best, but it wasn't ever good enough I have nothing left to give. I'm just dead inside and pretty shaken up. I feel I have been doing it alone. I can't fix us by myself while I can't even speak to you. I have reached out to hold you so many times and t when you said you didn't need a hand while getting your staples out just killed me. Why ask me to go with you?

Sorry.

Mac

His response—I got many responses, but this was the first one:

So does this mean that you are calling off the engagement/marriage . . . and breaking up with me again???

I am confused . . . why would you ask me to marry you if I was such an ass hole? And . . . then say yes to me when i proposed????

i feel like such a fucking dork! How am i going tell everybody . . . my daughters . . . my friends . . . my parents??? i feel like such a fucking looser!!!

At least your friends and family will be relieved and happy for you . . . that will make it much easier for you with all that support!!!

life goes on for you . . . i hope you find a guy who does give you the attention you are needing 24/7.

I didn't respond to that. For me it was over. I knew only my Monster could rescue himself, and now I had to rescue myself. The next few days were an ongoing of texts and e-mails back and forth. I was numb and didn't say much, but he was hurting, and letting me have it must have helped him. Almost a week later, I spoke with him on the phone. We had been texting about me getting his clothes and stuff back, and he told me to burn them. I thought that was pretty stupid. He had no money, and I had half of his stuff, so I got brave and decided to call him.

For some reason, I decided to tape the phone call, and I am so glad I did. For the first few minutes, he just called me names and said *fuck you* a lot. Then I asked him if I would ever get the money for Mexico back or the $1,150 I had lent him. He yelled, "No way. That's the price you pay for breaking up with me." I expected that, so I was staying pretty calm. Then I told him I was still going to continue to train for nationals and go to practices on weekends. He just blew.

He said, "Mark my words, you little bitch, you're not going to be there April 4. My friends hate you. They call you psycho bitch, and you will *not* be there."

My heart sank. I had been powerlifting to get my strength back. It wasn't about him; it was about me. I finally snapped and yelled back, "Listen here, you self-centered son of a bitch. I will be at nationals. You can't stop me!"

"Oh yes, I can. Mark my words, you won't be there!"

I hung up on him. That meet was my dream. I had worked forever for that day. I sat on my sofa, just sick. He took my heart, my money, my life, and now my dream too.

The phone rang about ten minutes later. I almost didn't answer, and then I noticed it was Lori, my Monster's powerlifter friend. She was calling about selling my house for me so my Monster and I could buy a farm. I never told her what was going on because she was his friend. Then she said this, "Sweetie, can I ask you if you're sure you want to do this?"

I said, "Yes, why do you ask?"

"Well, Bob and I can't figure this out. You seem like a really smart, together girl. Your home is amazing. You've travelled, and he has nothing. He's miserable 90 percent of the time, and we are kind of worried about you."

That was it; I burst into tears and told her almost everything. I never meant to, but I was such a mess. She guaranteed me that I'd be at practice and nationals, and they wouldn't let my Monster do anything to stop me.

With that, the war began! Believe it or not, the craziness hadn't really even started yet.

Shortly after, my dear friend Gerry called. He knew some of what had been going on, but I was such a mess, I told him everything. That's when he rescued me. He wanted to be my coach. He wanted to come to the gym every week and spot me so I could train. He would help me dress (the gear takes two people). He wanted to be at my side the entire meet so I wouldn't be intimidated. He asked nothing in return for this. Gerry and I are just friends, and he just did this to support me and for no other reason. My heart just melted. I couldn't believe he would help me this way. Most people were scared of my Monster, but Gerry didn't seem worried at all. I had called some of the other powerlifters, looking for a coach for the nationals, but everyone was afraid of the repercussions that my Monster would cause. It turned out many of the powerlifters hated him, but they knew better than to mess with him them too.

Gerry described my Monster as a bully. And he wasn't going to be bullied. He told me he thought that the following week my Monster would be kind of mean because he was hurting. Then the next week, he would be worse. Then after that, when he realized he had lost control of me, it would get even worse. Gerry was pretty much bang on, except it was more like months instead of weeks. Sometimes I wonder if it's going to be more like years.

Lori called me back after talking to Bob, president of our powerlifting federation, and told me that Bob wanted me at the meet. She also told me that she had never heard anyone say an unkind word about me. They often thought how my Monster was lucky to have me. It was so kind of her and Bob to say that as I actually believed it when my Monster said his friends called me psycho bitch. They rescued me that day too. They probably have no idea, but I was at rock bottom, playing my Monster's phone call over and over. And her phone call was the first step toward healing.

CHAPTER 10

Will I ever get my life back?

The following month was insanity of the purest kind. My Monster just lost it, and so did I. It was like we were back in grade 8, except more like war. He would e-mail and text me the most nasty things. I'd try to ignore him, but eventually, I'd break down and respond with something just as nasty. Hundreds of text messages. Some texts just said "Fuck Fuck Fuck." I never understood why he would do that.

One minute he wanted his ring back, and the next minute he was leaving me his ring in my gym bag. He was so threatening, it was just nuts. We would text sometimes for three hours straight. Never in my life was anything more insane, but I was just as much a part of it as he was.

His mom sent me an e-mail right after we broke up that told me she understood. She had always told him to be good to me and not mess this up. She had always told me that of all his girlfriends, I was her favorite. I loved her and still pray for her. Here is her last e-mail to me:

Hi Mckenzie,

How are you feeling? I hope you are better. Thanks for going to the doctors with him yesterday. I know he is feeling very low right now but I don't know what to do. He didn't give me much details on his foot except that he has a hard cast now. Did they say it seemed to be healing o.k. or is there something he has to do?

I know it is very hard times for the both of you and I hope you both can get through this. I wish you all the best. Please take care of yourself. I don't think anything can be done for my son.

Love Mary xoxo

During an afternoon of angry texting being sent back and forth with my Monster, he told me she hated me. I said that wasn't true as, just like Bob and Lori, she had been kind to me. They all knew he was miserable and knew that I had been tested in every way possible. His mother used to thank me for putting up with him. He hated that and used to complain that she liked me more than him. It was nuts. No one can love anyone more than your own son. I told him that, but he was treating his mom pretty cold when she would call, and it broke my heart. He had no idea what an amazing mom he had. He threatened to have his mom call me in one of the text messages. I told him to bring it on!

Much to my surprise, she did. She was mad and asked to me to leave her son alone. I tried to tell her that he texted me, and I had tried to ignore them for over thirty minutes. She called me a drama queen. That one made me kind of laugh. He called his mom to call his ex, and I'm the drama queen? Then she told me my dad had spoiled me rotten and still did to this day. I explained to her that my dad was amazing to me, and I refused to apologize to anyone for that, but she needed to know he'd been dead for five years. If he were alive, her son would have been dead. She settled down and just said please don't contact her son. I promised not to and wished her well. I couldn't believe he got his mom to call me. It hurt and hurt bad. Codependents can never handle rejection; it's like death for us.

Somehow getting his mom to call me made him feel better. In honesty, it made me feel better too. I was still worried about him, and I was glad to know she was sticking up for him. I hope she still is. He's pretty alone and needs all the help he could get. I never doubted that she wouldn't help him as she loved him so much.

It kind of backfired on him though. The support I had received from his friends and mine gave me a ton of strength. Shortly after his mom called me, my Monster sent me twenty-eight e-mails. I e-mailed every single one to his mom. I explained that I had not contacted him like she had asked, but this was what I received in the last hour and could she please call him and make him stop.

It actually stopped for about two days.

It didn't last long enough. He kept texting, saying how awful I was and what I'd done to him. The whole thing was insane! That's the only word I can use to describe it. The drama was just huge. Finally, we blocked each other in our e-mails. I would have changed my phone number too, but I used it for my business and couldn't. We were like two hurt little kids seeing who could hurt each other worse. I would try and ignore him, and then I would try and reason with him. That never worked. I'm not sure why I still tried. Eventually, I'd blow too.

Both our lives had been destroyed. I know my heart was completely crushed over and over and can safely assume he felt the same way. I was doing a diet for one of his clients, and she would tell me how he was doing. He totalled his truck and was really having a hard time. I was proud of myself for keeping him blocked at that time. I wanted to run to him and lend him money and make sure he was OK, but all I had to do was play that last phone call over, and I would smarten right up.

People would tell me he was walking on his foot, and I would worry because he wasn't allowed. I actually broke down and texted him about that at one point, but he told me to fuck off. That almost made me feel better. Insane as it sounds, his nastiness used to release me from caring or feeling guilty. I don't remember eating at all. I certainly wasn't sleeping. I wouldn't allow myself any wine or sleeping pills as I knew those would make things worse.

I trained like a crazy women; I was a crazy women. I poured my heart and soul into the nationals. The first time I went to a weekend practice with his friends, I was petrified. He'd scared me when he said I wasn't allowed to attend. I thought his friends might have been told nasty things about me and reject me. I sat in my truck before going in, just freaked out.

The practice was awesome. Everyone there was helping me. They acted like they liked me. No one gave a care about whether I was dating anyone or not. They saw that I loved powerlifting and busted their butts to help me. I learned more in eight weeks of practice than I had ever learned from my Monster. Those training days were my happy days.

Even Tom showed up to a practice and was nice to me. It was awkward between us at first, but then he told Lori that he would never judge me for breaking up with the Monster. I wanted to hug him and thank him for that. He is, and always will be, someone I greatly respect. We chatted and encouraged one another with our lifts. I think after dealing with the Monster and his chaos for so long, I expected everyone to find fault in me, but as the weeks progressed, I started to learn that I was not so bad.

I was working at the gym where the Monster and I trained together. The owner's son, who ran the place, started giving me client after client. What a lifesaver he was to me. It was really helping to pay my debts back. I even managed to pay for my bedroom wall to be fixed. My clients were all losing weight, and word got around that I was a good trainer, and my clientele was really growing. God must have been answering my prayers; one client hired me because she saw how much fun I had with my clients. I thought I must be recovering from my dark days. I was still brokenhearted, but I was doing a lot better.

I even put myself back on the dating website. It was dumb, and I wasn't ready, but I was trying to fill my time with anything other than thoughts of my Monster. I met a nice guy. I almost didn't go meet him when I heard his name, which was the same as the Monster. He's a master soccer player and worked out every day. Our first date was training in the gym. We laughed; I laughed. It was fun. I only allowed myself to see him every week or so. He's another pretty boy, and that scares me too. Actually, everything scares me. I have put him through every test I can think of. His ex-girlfriends aren't crazy, so he passed that test. I think if you have one crazy ex that's OK, but if all of them are nuts, it says a lot about you. I learned that Monster's exes weren't crazy on their own accord. My soccer player had a stable job as a nurse in a brain injury unit and owned his home. I think by the time we are forty, we should be stable, or maybe we will never be. I was considering dating this guy until one night over dinner, he told me his parents had divorced when he was young and some of his mom's boyfriends made his childhood pretty tough. This time, instead of feeling sorry for him, I red-flagged it. I had my eye on that because Little Ms. Codependent wasn't going to rescue anyone!

Next I met Brad. He's awesome. We talked every single day, sometimes twice. I know I went to the dating site far too soon, but I can honestly say he had made a huge difference in my life. He listened to me whine and carry on, or maybe he watched the hockey game and didn't listen, but either way, every night he called and put up with me as I got through everything. I was not sure where it would go, but I have to say, he seemed to be one of the kindest men I had ever met. He kind of reminded me of my ex-boyfriend before my Monster, a man I will always admire and respect. It was too soon, and for no reason, I had to bolt, but it was step in a direction away from the Monster, so I don't regret it.

CHAPTER 11

Oh, I walk through the valley of death.

The texting and e-mails only got worse. I believed the Monster was taking his painkillers that he'd gotten from the hospital but, of course, don't know for sure. All I knew was his depression was worse than ever. The closer we got to nationals, the more threatening he became. I trained an insane amount just to try to cope. It was so hard to ignore his constant name-calling and threats. He still worked at my gym, but most of his clients were gone. He started training himself at my gym, and that made my life a living hell.

Most days he was just rude, kicking my gym bag, snickering at me when I tried to train my clients. My clients were scared of him. I tried so hard to hold my head high and just keep doing my job as I desperately needed the money. Some days he was sad and crying. They were actually the worst because those days my guilt strings were pulled. I had to fight myself so hard to just ignore him and go forward, never backward. All my thoughts were consumed of him as he was seeing me every day, and when he wasn't at the gym, he was texting or e-mailing. I was so exhausted I hardly remember what was going on.

I had been training a friend of mine who was a nurse in a psyche ward. She had known me throughout my time with my Monster. She was always bugging me to reach out for help. She used to see my texts from the Monster as I was training her. Fortunately, she had the knowledge to realize just how sick he was getting. The texts that were once just swear words had turned to death threats. Once he learned I was training for nationals and planning on breaking my records without him, he was beyond livid. No one was allowed to do well without him. In his mind, no one could. I think it drove him crazy that my life was carrying on. I have to admit, the texts were starting to scare me. I had an alarm installed, and so did my mother. He would text all the details as to how I would die because that was what I deserved.

That little nurse saved my life. One afternoon, I was training her, and as usual, his nonstop texting began again. She dragged me into the office and wouldn't let up on me to call the police. Then she took me for lunch and begged me to call for help. I was petrified to call the police as I knew the Monster would get into trouble. I would never ever do that to him. I went home thinking about calling. The texts stopped for thirty minutes. Then the doorbell rang. Like an idiot, I answered it. There stood my Monster, uglier than ever. He looked thinner and drugged up. I was terrified. I clicked a button on my alarm that sent a silent alarm to the police to come quick. I can still see myself pushing the button. It was so hard, but I knew I had no choice. I won't go into detail about that day, but to tell you, it took eighteen minutes for the police to show up, and by then he had bolted. All I know was that was the day I learned to beg and plead for my life.

The police came in my house and interviewed me. I didn't tell them much as I was still protecting my Monster. They held my cell phone and read his messages as they came in. They told me I needed to go the shelter and be safe. I don't recall being given much of a choice. I recall a text the police received that talked about how he would hang me for what I had done to him.

My children went to their dad's, my cats went with a client, and off I went for my first trip to the Calgary Women's Emergency Shelter. I remember it was dinnertime. I remember having a grocery bag of clothes and my meds. I remember everything being all blurry. I had been taking as many sports supplement drugs as I could find that were legal as the nationals was only two weeks away. I had more protein and creatine and amino acids than I did underwear. They were all that mattered to me. I was as mentally unstable as I had ever been.

We got to the door and gave a password through a speaker, and I stepped inside. Then I had to give another password to get into the second door. As the second door crashed behind me, I shook. I felt I was going to pass out. I was greeted by a caseworker who took me to a tiny room with two twin beds. I knew she gave me tons of information, but I don't remember any of it. I don't know if I even spoke to her. I just crawled into the tiny bed and curled into fetal position. I can't even tell you if the lights were on or off. I recall taking my first deep breath. I think I had been holding my breath for six months. I was able to process that I was safe, and I could just stop everything. I slept and slept and slept. People kept coming and checking on me, but I can't recall anything they said. I slept for three days in my little fetal position.

On day 3, the police wanted to talk to me, and my mother had been calling nonstop, so I had to get out of bed. I talked to my hysterical mom and told her I was safe. I asked her to call my Monster and make sure he was safe. (I was nuts, remember?)

Two young police officers interviewed me in a tiny room. I wanted to go home, but they insisted I was right where I needed to be. I was mad. This place was hell. They took all my drugs away and only gave me what I needed when they decided. I couldn't train. I remember doing bicep and triceps work with phone books and water bottles. I'd do push-ups till I dropped. I felt like I was in prison. The women that were in there were idiots. They sat around, telling their stupid stories and crying all the time. They made me crazy, and I hated them almost as much as I hated the staff.

I didn't need to be there. I wasn't abused. I wasn't poor. I had a home for goodness' sake. I don't think I had ever been so angry. To top it off, I was gaining weight. I was going out of my mind. All I wanted to do was go home and check on my Monster. No one would listen to me. I would go to my little bedroom and just scream out of the sheer agony of being trapped in there.

My roommate was a nightmare, such a cry baby. I remember treating her a bit like my Monster had treated me. The place was the single worst place I had ever been. They made me eat horrible food like bagels and beef. You see, I had been on a high-protein bodybuilding diet for months and hated anything normal. I had forgotten what normal was and didn't care to remember.

They forced me to see a counselor. That day I will never forget. My caseworker led me through seVernal hallways, passing more weeping women, and into a dimly lit tiny room. In walked Verna. I'm guessing twenty-four years old. I snickered thinking *How the hell is this kid going to help me?* I hated her. In my mind, she was a little blond bimbo that knew nothing of my life. Somehow I got the idea that maybe if I worked with her, she could get me out.

She had pencil, crayons, and colored paper and said we were going to do some art therapy. I'm embarrassed to admit I said this; I'm pretty sure I told her what she could do with her art therapy using language that was more than colorful. She only smiled and kept right on talking. I didn't intimidate her in the least. It was like little Verna had met someone like me before. She drove me crazy. She drew circles on a page and put my parents name in them and asked a million questions about my past. I thought it was stupid. We needed to help the Monster, not discuss my parents. She never stopped with all her ridiculous questions. Then she said, "Well, Ms. Brown, you are the classic codependent." She seemed all proud of herself. I was ticked right off and explained to her that I was dependent on no one and never been. I resented being called that horrible word. You see, I didn't know the meaning of the word. She smiled and let me rant, telling her she had no idea who I was. Then she said, "Well now, you are going to learn to depend on me. I am going to help you. I am going to hold your hand and get you back on your feet. You're not allowed to be codependent around this place." I walked out very frustrated but, admittedly, thinking a bit about what she had said as she described what a codependent was.

My therapy had begun, and it was about time. I spent every afternoon with Verna and learned so much. I was allowed to go out with an escort and train at a gym. Then I got to take short walks and buy myself a coffee. I talked to my mom and kids every day. For the first time ever, I was working on myself.

I was finally released from the shelter. I stayed at Mom's for a few days, but she was so scared of the Monster, I thought it best to leave. I moved in with my friend Gerry for a while just to feel safe. For the most part, I did feel safe. He wasn't allowed to contact me, which gave me the ability to rest, something I needed most of all.

Nationals came and went. Gerry coached me through it, and I took three gold medals, breaking all the Canadian records. The Monster was there, but I was under a protective order, so he couldn't speak to me. I have to admit, seeing him was tough, but I stayed focused on my lifts. I used techniques Verna had taught me, to use his intimidation tactics to gather strength. The more he stood staring at me, the heavier I lifted. As I did my final dead lift, he came right out on stage and glared me down. When you dead lift, your breathing is done in a certain way to give you strength. I didn't do any of my breathing. I reached down and grabbed my bar with a suicide grip. I never took my eyes off the Monster, and as I lifted the bar, a world-record lift that has never been broken to this day, I mouthed the words *fuck you!* As the bar crashed to the mat, the audience went crazy. The first four rows were filled with all the friends I thought I had lost.

Everyone was there except my mom. She had taken a trip to the United States with her sisters that had been booked since the previous year. My godmother took her place and took photos from the front row. I had no idea just how much of my mom she would be replacing in the future. I phoned Mom as soon as I finished, and she cried; she was so happy for me. I had done it. Most of all, I had done it without the Monster.

I was standing around the auditorium, chatting with some friends after my final lift when I felt a strange quiver in my lower abdomen. The Monster had left after I made my dead lift, so I was feeling pretty good. Then I felt the quiver again. I told my daughter that I must have torn an abdominal muscle lifting or something. Then she put her hand on my stomach and said she could feel it too. I tried to ignore it, thinking perhaps it was a result of all the sports supplements I had taken earlier that day. As I was leaving the auditorium, I felt it again. It hit me. The only time I had ever felt this was when I was pregnant. I laughed at myself knowing that couldn't be true as I had an IUD and hadn't been intimate with the Monster since January, and it was now April 4. I put that thought out of my mind. I dropped my daughter with her dad and went out to party and celebrate my medal with my friends. I tried drinking but felt sick and then tired. I kept getting that strange quiver in my stomach.

I went home early. As I walked in the door, I couldn't ignore it anymore. I remember getting on my knees in my living room and praying as hard as I could. "I can't be pregnant, God. I can't do it. I hate the Monster. Please, God, don't let this be so."

The next morning, I did a home pregnancy test. Sure enough, I was pregnant. I think I went into shock as I saw the results were positive. I cried this strange eerie cry that sounded like a dying dog. I literally howled. It came from so far in my body that it was like nothing I had ever heard before. I was adopted and was dead against abortion, but I did not want his baby inside of me. I don't know how long I cried. I think the rest of the day. It's still a blur to this day.

I saw my doctor the following morning. He really felt I should terminate the pregnancy. I had been on so many sports supplements that the odds of it being a viable fetus were slim. I also still had the IUD inside me. He went on to tell me about children being born with an IUD attached to their heads. I was numb once again as he pushed for an abortion. I wanted my mom, but she was still in the States.

The next day, I had an ultrasound. I was almost four months pregnant. I couldn't believe it. How could I not have known? The baby seemed fine. I was told if you have an IUD and lose a large amount of weight, it could move, and you can get pregnant. My weight had been yo-yoing for a year with what I was putting it through. I never once thought of telling the Monster I was just enjoying not hearing from him.

I met with Verna twice a week, but that week it was three times. She was very supportive and really understood how hard the decision was for me to make. It took a few days, but I decided I was going to give birth to it. I called it *It* as it wasn't real to me. I went back to work and tried to carry on, not sure what I was going to do. I saw the Monster at my gym but just ignored him. I would not even acknowledge that he was in the room. I had to take care of It, not him. Oh, he tried to be a jerk, stealing my weights, etc, but for the most part, it never fazed me.

I told Mom of my disaster the moment she came home. It was Good Friday in fact. I had actually started writing this book the day before. Verna had me reading through my journal as part of my therapy, and it had inspired the good little codependent in me to write a book to help other women with their own Monsters. At noon, I started spotting. By two, I was bleeding bad and was having terrible cramps. I decided to go to the gym and ignore it. The pain became too great. I called Mom, and she met me at the same hospital I went to when the Monster had been beat up.

In honesty, I think I knew I was having a miscarriage. I had had that before but never this far along. They did an ultrasound and decided a D and C was out of the question as It was too big. I was forced to deliver. They gave me an intravenous drip to speed it up and then some jelly to help open my cervix fully. The pain was awful. The emotions were so weird. I didn't want It, but I also knew It was mine and a victim like me. Then I would think about the life It would have knowing a father like my Monster. I stopped and prayed between contractions and asked God to take It to heaven. I explained that I couldn't be a good mother and that I wanted him to parent for me. I begged him to take care of It. Mom and I prayed together that It would be spared of ever knowing the Monster. It was born at 7:22. It was a boy. They packed little It up and took him away. I saw him and held It. I never cried; I was very strong or numb—one of the two. Perhaps it was my imagination, but I swear I saw the Monster's face.

Two days later, Mom and I took It's ashes to our old farm and spread It with my dad. As we sent It's ashes flying, I remember saying "I will see you soon, my son." And that was the one and only time I ever called It my child. It was Easter Sunday. We followed our private funeral for It with a Chinese buffet, and I slept over at my mom's. Little did I know the worst was yet to come.

Chapter 12

When one door closes, another one opens.

I remember the next few days being a blur. My hemoglobin was low and so was my mind-set. I assumed I was back in fetal position. The past few weeks had been so hard to understand. The protective order had lifted, and I was back getting texts from my Monster. They didn't faze me much, and I never responded to any of them. I didn't even think of It very often. I think denial worked best for me at that time. The Monster was still at my gym, but I hardly noticed him there and only went because I had clients who needed the still very codependent me.

I had started kickboxing with a client I had done nutrition work for. I never took it too seriously, but it was a tremendous release. I punched the heavy bag like only a girl can.

My daughter Paige and husband Kale were two months from having their second baby. I decided to try and focus on the baby coming and to make a small attempt at becoming happy. Paige called just after lunch one day to tell me her water had broke. I just couldn't believe it. She was only thirty-three weeks pregnant. Was I really going to lose this too? Did God hate me or something? Was this the punishment I deserved for not looking after the Monster?

My grandson Able was born at six pounds four ounces. The delivery was horrific as my precious daughter tried desperately to hang on to the tiny life that had been growing inside her. I was needed at the hospital as Kale was desperate for some support. There I was back in that awful hospital I had just walked out of. How on earth could this be happening so soon after losing It?

The strangest things went through my mind. I saw the same nurses since Able was delivered on the same unit as It. In honesty, I think I was so far in mental fetal position that I was there in a physical sense only. I knew I hated that horrible hospital. I put on my codependent face and decided to make those few days all about my daughter and son-in-law. I was needed. Once again, from the depths, the codependent ran to help. I am positive I could have explained to them that I had just lost It, and they would have found other people to help them. The guilt a codependent carries would have rather died than not be available or, God forbid, ask for help for myself.

Able was in a very serious condition. We really weren't sure if he would even survive. His little diaper had blood inside as his organs was still struggling to grow. He was on a breathing machine and spent his days in a tiny covered incubator just trying to live. We couldn't touch him or love him. It was awful. My little Paige cried and cried as she begged God to spare this child. I spent a fair amount of time at the hospital trying to help. I never tried to hold our little Able as it was all too unbearable.

My mother had caught a nasty cold while travelling in the United States, so she wasn't allowed to meet her new great-grandson for fear of spreading the infection. I would phone her each time I left the hospital to try and keep her updated to his condition. Being at the hospital so much was a bit of a break because I had to have my phone turned off, and the Monster couldn't get to me. I could turn the phone on when I reached the dreaded parkade and get all his texts for the day at once and simply hit delete. It had been over two months since I got him out of my home, but nothing had really changed as to how much contact he made since the protective order lifted. I recall thinking any day, he would just go away.

We still shared a few clients, so occasionally, I'd get updates as to what chaos he had found next. As usual, his life was continuing in the same pattern I had shared with him. Life was always insane for the Monster.

I was supposed to have Sunday dinner with my mother, which was our normal routine. Since my father had passed three years earlier, we tried to have Sunday Chinese buffet together. On this particular Sunday, she suggested I not come. Her cold had worsened and didn't want me risking passing her cold to Able. I agreed to miss out on our Sunday chicken balls.

I spent most of Sunday night at the hospital with my Paige and Able. He had a very tough night with his alarms going off constantly. We got so used to the machines in his room going off that we started to almost ignoring them. My ex-husband and his new wife had come to visit that evening. I watched as my children's father looked deeply into the eyes of his lovely new wife with such passion. I saw him holding her hand and caring for her with so much admiration. It hurt and felt like he had never loved me that way. I didn't leave the room or allow my heart some space so I hurt less. Instead I happily chatted with them both and congratulated them on their newfound love. Once again the codependent never ever looked after herself, only the people I was surrounded by. It wasn't about me; it was about Paige, so I had to be strong. I'd spend hours with Paige and never once told her of my pain. It was as though if I talked about, it would be real. That way I could stay in fetal position.

CHAPTER 13

The woman who always loved me was gone in the
blink of an eye.

The phone rang early. It was an ambulance attendant explaining that they were taking my mom to the hospital where Paige and Able were. I couldn't believe it. I had just left. Apparently, Mom was having trouble breathing, so she had called for help. I jumped in the truck and ran yet again to that horrible place. It was surreal. I ran there just like when the Monster got beat up one day. I ran there again when It died then ran there again when Able was born, and now I was running there for my mom. I just couldn't believe this was happening again or was still happening. *Will this nightmare never end?* I asked myself as I entered the dreaded parkade from hell. The parking attendants were all becoming familiar to me. It was just too much for one very lonely and lost little girl to bear.

I went to the emergency department, but the doctors wouldn't let me inside. If I had gone to visit my mother, it would have meant not being able to go back into the neonatal intensive care with Able. Her doctor spoke to me and explained that she had a chest infection and that she was going to be just fine. He asked me to arrange a ride home for her as she would be released after her chest X-ray came back. The doctor was kind enough to allow me to speak with my mom on the phone.

Mom reassured me that staying outside was the best thing to do. She was embarrassed to have panicked and called an ambulance, and that she would be just fine. She asked me to call her next door neighbor and arrange for her ride back to Okotoks where she lived. Mom sounded well, and I let out a sigh of relief.

I spent the morning with Paige and my grandson as he had experienced yet another difficult night. It was all getting the best of my exhausted daughter, so I had to be with her instead of my mom. I went back to check on my mother around 11:00 AM. She was still doing well, but no one had time to get us each a phone. I passed a note to her with a security guard; it read, "Hey, Mom, I'm off to work now. Baby's doing OK. I'll call you tonight."

Mom wrote back, "Chin up, kiddo. Love you. Don't worry about me."

I sped back to the gym to train two clients. I think, for the most part, no one at my work had any idea what a mess I was in other than perhaps the owner, who worked behind the desk. She was a kind lady a few years younger than my mom. She knew a bit about the Monster because he worked there too, but she seemed to always ask how I was. That was kind. I have never forgotten that. I was so alone in my world of codependency that the only person that came near me was behind a front desk at my gym. Oh, I had friends, but life had been so insane, I shut out everyone. My days were filled with helping Paige, getting Mandy and Branden to school, working, deleting Monster's texts and e-mails, and sleeping up to three hours a night. And I start the same crazy routine all over again the next morning.

My cell phone had rang several times during my last client of the afternoon. I didn't answer it because I knew I would soon be done working. I had planned to return home at three o'clock and be there for Branden's return from school. I would return any phone calls at that time and maybe get an hour's sleep before returning for five more hours of work in the evening.

I wrapped up my client and hopped in the truck to check my phone. I was shocked to hear the doctor's voice on my voice mail. He told me to come back to the hospital quickly as my mother's condition had changed, and she was rapidly declining. He suggested I bring her family. I was in complete disbelief. It all made no sense once again. I grabbed Branden from school and drove yet again to the dreaded hospital. I left messages for the other children and phoned a client of all things. I asked her if she could call the Monster and see if he would take my evening clients. That may sound insane after all he and I had been through. I learned later through counselling that I did that because he was what I had known for so many months before. As I pulled into the parkade from hell, my client returned my call and told me that the Monster had said "Tell her to go to hell." As usual, it was all about him and never about me. No matter how bad my crisis was, he would never be there; I just hadn't learned that yet.

I quickly called my clients and cancelled their sessions, promising a free session the next day. Once again crazy, I know. Branden and I went into emergency department to be with Mom. The doctor said she needed me more than my grandson, so the decision to be by her side was easy.

She was puffed up like a balloon. Branden was very shaken up seeing her so ill. I arranged for his dad to get him out of there as I was so worried about my little boy. The doctors had no clue what was happening to my mother. Her organs were shutting down and for no reason whatsoever. Mikayla and Mandy helped me as they settled her into intensive care. We were all in shock, but I think I appeared very in control. Thank goodness I had learned mental fetal position, or I am sure I would have had a nervous breakdown. In honesty, I wish I could have just passed out and not watch the next twelve hours unfold.

I spoke with my mom, who no longer looked like my mom. She asked me to put on her diamond earrings that she had been wearing. I promised not to lose them. She told me not to worry, that she would be OK. She wanted water as her mouth was dry. The girls all looked to me for answers. We stayed in touch with Paige, which was easy as she was just a couple of floors up with her sick little boy.

The doctors told me that she needed exploratory surgery as she was dying, and they didn't know why. I was scared as she had always requested a do-not-resuscitate order be in place. I couldn't bear having her die, so I agreed to the surgery. I sat alone and explained to her why I had agreed to this. I told her I was selfish and couldn't possibly live without her. I was crying and apologizing when she squeezed my hand three times. We had always done that since I was a little girl. One of us squeezed three times and the other squeezed four times. It meant "I love you" and "I love you too." Even though she couldn't speak, I knew I had her blessing to make these decisions on her behalf.

She came out of surgery worse than before. She looked far worse and couldn't communicate at all. I sat numbly in a tiny waiting room with my daughters. Paige had joined us. Three of my mom's dear friends had come to see us. Each one spent a few minutes with her. My godmother came too. She tried to prepare me for what was coming, but I hardly remember her speaking because I just wouldn't hear of it. The girls chatted as we waited, but I have no recollection of the words being said. I remember crazy things instead, like there was a photo of Alberta roses on the wall and a cheap veneer-covered coffee table and a pink sofa. The minute seemed like days.

My mom had so many machines and IVs connected to her, it was like something out of a horror film. I counted nineteen different bags being pumped into her. I recall demanding to know what each one was. Why? I have no idea. The doctor kindly explained everything to me, and the bottom line was, they were trying anything they could but failing miserably. My mom was dying.

I asked for time alone with her and made my girls wait outside. I took my mom's hands in mine and told her if she didn't get herself better, I'd go marching right back to the Monster. I knew that would surely work as no one hated him more than she did.

I didn't work; nothing worked, no matter how hard I prayed or begged or pleaded—nothing. She just got worse. Then the doctors and some other people came to our tiny waiting room with the ugly pink sofa and told us we had to turn off the life support. It was just after midnight. When they left, my three little girls looked at me like I would have some answer that could bring Grandma back. I was the caregiver, the fixer, the doer—a.k.a. codependent—and I was not expected to fail. Mac never failed. I could fix and do anything even to my own demise, but this I could not fix. It was truly the lowest moment of my life. I never ever had an experienced anything worse than those few hours of waiting for a miracle.

I retreated to my parkade from hell for a cigarette. The lonely dark walk to the truck hadn't been as scary as the first time. I'd done it weeks before when the Monster was mad at me because he had been beat up. I sat in the truck and thought about everything. My crazy Monster and how I had loved him so. My sick grandson, my dead baby, my stressed-out son-in-law. My broken son left to worry about his grandma without me there, but most of all, I thought about turning off the life support and letting my mom go. For the first time in my life, I finally reached out for help. Perhaps my codependency was broken. I actually admitted I couldn't do this alone. I grabbed for my cell phone and called my Monster. You ask, why did I call him? I really thought he was the only one that could help me.

He answered the phone in a sleepy, grumpy voice. I was crying hard and breathing heavy. I told him that Mom was dying, and they were turning off her life support soon, and that I needed him to come and be by my side. I begged in fact, and it was very hard for me to do.

He actually laughed at me and said, "Good, you little bitch, you are getting exactly what you deserve for leaving me." Then he hung up. I just sat there, silent; I didn't even cry. I had never asked anyone for help in my whole life, and that was the response God had allowed. It was the darkest moment of my entire life.

CHAPTER 14

*The footprints in the sand were many as I was carried
through the next few weeks.*

After several more hours of delaying the inevitable, I called to my ex-husband, and he ran to the hospital to help. He was a saint as he led in prayer and song when my mom left us and journeyed to be with my dad.

I remember feeling so alone. So much about the next month was surreal. My eldest daughter stayed by my side. I mean even sleeping with me. Paige helped with what she could but still had a sick baby to contend with, only now without me. I don't think I saw Able for several weeks. My Mandy started phoning everyone and becoming a caregiver too. I argued back and forth with my only brother as he didn't come to the hospital to see my mother nor did he want to go to her funeral. I had to make autopsy decisions and cremation preparations. It was just overwhelming. Everyone had different opinions except me. I didn't have an opinion on anything. I was just dumb, in a fog far thicker than I had ever experienced. I was very fortunate to have the friends I did. Its amazing how you really learn who cares about you at times like that. I had a client at my Gym whom I'd been training for several months. She rushed in and took my dog Jack for me when I went to the shelter. She stared down my monster every chance she got. I hardly knew Tina when all this started but by the end I loved her and she loved me. I will never forget how she ran to my rescue. Not to mention how she has helped with my website.

The Monster, now called the Evil One, was texting, but I can't tell you what any of them said. I had just left the planet. I think I went into a cocoon where no one could get to me and slept there.

I put this chapter in this book to show you that you're not alone even when you think you are. You see, my Mikayla took over; she became the adult. She wrote obituaries, planned the service, and ordered death certificates. She just stepped up to the plate. My Paige called every few hours to check on me. My Mandy fed us all and spread the news. They all looked after Branden and saw that he was held and taught about grief and missing his grandma. My best friend Gerry called hourly and visited often to see that I was OK. My pals Ronnie and Tony brought food and visited for hours. They talked for hours, but I have no idea what we talked about. Life was insane around me, and all I remember doing was looking out the window and missing my mom. Flowers were showing up, and there was food and baking. I just sat there in silence, like a dead person. Somehow, the few people I had left in my life just walked in and took over. They chose songs, organized a choir, found her favorite hymns, and made slide shows, and I just sat there.

The codependent couldn't even help herself, let alone anyone else. It sounds like a horrible time, and it was. The worst. I still cry when I think back, but I learned something very important, and if you are in a shelter reading this, I want you to think about this. It's important; it could save your life.

I learned the following:

It's OK to let someone rescue you.

It's OK to ask for help.

People will actually show up and help.

You're worthy of someone helping.

You're never really alone unless you chose to be.

And most of all, no matter how bad it is, as long as you still have air in your lungs, you will be OK. Time heals all wounds. (I hate that quote, but it's so true.)

CHAPTER 15

I found anger, and I liked it!

After months of counseling with Verna and starting training my Muay Thai (full-contact martial arts and kickboxing) with Darryl (my trainer), I finally struck back. It wasn't to get even; it was to prove to myself that I could. So much had gone wrong. But the entire time, I had kept being happy little Mac, smiling every day and pretending to have control of things. The Evil One was still walking around the gym being mean. He was still putting me down to everyone. I thought I was being the bigger person by not doing this to him, but all I did was deny myself the truth I felt. Sometimes turning the other cheek only gives an abuser another side to hit.

For the most part, I understood. He was hurt, but so was I. In him there are two people: the scared little boy with the screwed up past (that's the one I loved) and the huge grump who could only be angry and miserable rather than honest and real with himself (that's the one I grew to hate). I was doing really well at being over our disaster of a relationship was even dealing with my mom's death better than I expected. I did go visit the little graveside I made for our baby on my father's farm often, but that was just on really sad, lonely Sunday afternoons. My business was growing far beyond what I ever expected, keeping me very busy. Life had almost returned to normal, except for when I was at the gym with him.

I didn't make eye contact for fear of falling apart. Some days it was fear, and others it was just hurt and heartbreak. Knowing he was there made me think of the baby and, most of all, the horrible things he had said to me when Mom died and when I bought the wrong oranges, when I knew the way to nationals, or God forbid, when I learned I had a fat ass. It would all go through my head when I had to share a room with him. Prior to my mom's passing, I used to make daily boundaries. At first I'd say "OK, if he calls to apologize, he can come back to my life." The next week, it would be "OK, if he calls, apologizes, and agrees to get help, he can come back into my life." The following week, it would be "OK, if he calls and agrees to get help after six months, he can come back." Those boundaries kept me strong, and of course, he never called other than to tell me what a horrible person I was. After Mom died, which was when I asked for help, I never needed another boundary again. Nothing he could have said or done would have allowed him in my life. I did, however, need to get angry to finally get through the mess he had helped make of my life.

I had learned that when I met the Evil One, my life was happy and pink. Then it got dark gray, then blackish, some days purple, but in the end, it would be very, very black. As I grew and learned, I realized his life had been black for years before he met me. That gave me the knowledge to set a goal to make my life pink again. It gave me permission to be happy and have peace in my life. It gave me a guilt-free ticket to stop caring about rescuing the Evil One. It taught me (this was a lightbulb moment) that I couldn't rescue him nor did I have to. I was allowed to go back on my word and not rescue him. With that came yet another revelation, another new emotion for Mac: it was hate. I have often expressed that *hate* was not a big enough word to describe what I felt for the Evil One.

One night, a client we both shared told me that the Evil One had told her husband that I had played him. That I just went around collecting engagement rings and never cared about him at all. At first I laughed, and then I cried. How could he think that? I wondered. Yes, I had a small collection going on, but didn't he know that he was the only man I had ever said yes to, including my ex-husband? Didn't he know that I thought of him as my soul mate? Surely, he knew that I had once loved him like no other. As usual, it was insane. I went to sleep that night knowing he would always be sad or angry. That he would never be happy like me. Misery was all he ever knew.

I kept hearing Darryl's (my kickboxing trainer) voice telling me to stop showing fear. Then Verna saying "You need to get angry and stand up for yourself." I was so sick and tired of hearing about him from his friends, I was ready to be scream. I was sick of seeing him too. The kind, gentle person I once knew was gone. That side of him hadn't shown up often when we were together, but now that we were apart, he was truly gone for good. I had enough. I never knew that I could be pushed too far, but it had happened.

I knew if Darryl was going to get me in the ring, I had to overcome my fear and get angry. I knew Verna was right about my not getting mad. So I did just that. I stood up from the fetal position I had been hiding in. I went after him the only way I knew how. I texted him and told him he had to pay me back some of the money he owed me. Oh, I was swearing and ranting like a crazy woman. He accused me of being as crazy as his ex, but I told him I was far crazier. I threatened to tell his dad all he'd done if he didn't pay me. I actually played the father card. The one I swore I never would. I was tired of babying him. I think I was angry about being alone for the end of our baby at Easter. I didn't tell him because I feared his nasty comments, and I knew he would be really angry that I was that far along. Even in that troubled time, I had been protecting him for fear of upsetting him.

This time he was getting treated the way he treated me. Kind of like how nasty he was when I reached out the night Mom was dying. I was getting even and then some. I wanted him to hurt and worried and maybe fearful. I swear if I had seen him that night, I would have walked right up to him and give him my left jab, then my right hook, which is slowly becoming my best weapon. Then I would have stomped on his injured foot as hard as I could. At the time, I wondered who this woman was. I had never wanted to hurt anyone in my life, but oh, how I wanted him to feel what he had done to me. I knew going after him would make him really mad, but because of my time at the kickboxing studio, I learned that he was a bully just full of words. I had learned that men who act the way he does only belittle the weak; they fear the strong. They are like Chinese pugs who think they are pit bulls.

I had never been a fighter; I had been the peacemaker and the girl in defense mode doing damage control in my crumbling little world, but that day, I put fear away and just went after him. I was the pit bull! All five foot two of me! I'm glad I didn't do it to him in person because I know I would have started hitting him and not been able to stop.

Much to my surprise, my VibePlate was in my driveway the next day, and I got postdated checks the day after. I had to laugh. He was still telling people I was crazy, but that made me laugh too because, for the first time, I wasn't crazy. I was strong physically and mentally, and I had proved it to myself. I trained with Darryl for three hours that night, and he kept saying "I don't know what happened, but you're a different girl tonight." He knocked me down and hit me in the head countless times, but I bounced right back and went after him. My shoulder and back were throbbing, but I didn't want to stop.

I wasn't done showing my power yet. I texted the Evil One back and went after him for money for our trip to Mexico. It was like winning a fight in the first round after you train for months. I still wanted more. He had given in so much easier than I expected. He was freaking out, telling me to call my lawyer and sue him. I considered playing the dad card again but decided that was hitting below the belt. I was more than even when I did it for the first time. I wanted him to hurt like he had made me hurt, but I didn't want to become anything like him.

My final text to him was "LOL, you never really knew me at all." How quickly he forgot the girl that brought him breakfast in bed every single day, even when she was sick. How quickly he forgot the girl that ran to the hospital for him in the middle of the night when he got beat up (chapter 5). How quickly he forgot the support I gave him in Cranbrook (chapter 4). How quickly he forgot that I give money to all kinds of people in trouble. I had even offered him money since we had broken up. The whole thing was just funny.

I had enough money of my own to almost retire as Mom had left me all the money I had invested in the farm. I drove home from the gym, laughing and thinking *Why the hell would he think I would take his stupid fifty-dollar postdated checks—that would be a pain for the next three years*. I knew he was in trouble; money hadn't exactly been kind to him the way it had me. As if I would take a dime of his money when

I had been blessed with so much? He even told one of his guy friends that he was worried I would take my inheritance and get a hotshot lawyer and go after him. It was the usual insanity. Even if I had, what would I have gotten? He had nothing, not because he wasn't capable of having anything because he was one of the hardest workers I knew, but because he only believed on gloom and doom and hated himself so bad that he would sabotage anything good that was starting in his life. I tried to help him many times with his business, but it would just fall on deaf ears. I don't think he could bear taking advice from anyone as it meant someone knew something he didn't. He was so busy being negative and miserable; I don't think he ever even knew me.

He still hates my guts, and some days, that emotion crops up for me too. I remember to my dad saying "You can't hate who you don't love." We must have loved each other a lot to hate each other the way we did, but it no longer mattered. I stood up to him, and his power over me was gone for good. Oh, I still cared about him and probably always will, but it's in the past now. I'm sure I will always worry about how he's doing, but it's not the same anymore. He's no longer mine to rescue, not that anyone ever is. He will never see the love I had for him because he can only see the bad. What a bizarre mix we were. Me, who only saw the good, and him, who only saw the bad. It would have been nice if we could have balanced each other out as we were both pretty screwed up. That day would never come.

I gave him back his silly checks with a copy of this chapter of the book. This little life lesson was about me, not him, and it was long overdue. For one brief second, I fantasized that he would come to me and say he would try, and we would get help for us both. He would say he missed me the way I had missed him, and by some huge miracle, we would learn to get along and ride happily ever after into the sunset. Then I laughed, thinking yin and yang would have a better chance finding harmony. He was black, and I was white, and there was no chance.

Things did, however, change for me. I can walk in the gym with my usual smile, but this time it's almost real, like it was before I met him. My eggshells were gone and so was the power he once had over me. I had loved, hurt, and been healed, finally! I knew I would never be the same after the past eighteen months but promised to only focus on the positive. I have less trust now, which will hopefully make me wiser. I'm stronger now, which must be a good thing. I love powerlifting as much as the first time I did it, and no one can stop me from doing it. I have never competed again, but perhaps one day, I will. I love fighting too, and no one can stop me from that either. I doubt I would have ever done either without first walking on eggshells, so I'm grateful for every last bit of it!

The best part about right now is that I will never walk on eggshells again. The next male to call me fat ass or anything else cruel and nasty is going to regret it, big time. Never again will I cater to bad behavior. Never again will I try to rescue anyone. Never again will I feel responsible for some fool who still hangs on to his childhood like it was yesterday. Never again will I tolerate someone who has to live in constant chaos because my life is happy and good, and it's been a long road back. I had learned to rescue myself at long last instead of worrying about everyone else. It didn't happen without amazing support from the Calgary Women's Emergency Shelter, my amazing children (thank God they put their foot down), my Ronnie, my Gerry, and my Tony who never stopped loving me as I fumbled from one disaster to another discovering my codependency.

Journal entry:

June 14, 2009

I've had an awesome day. Peaceful might be the best word to describe it. It's weird to feel good. I went for a 45 min run really early before it got hot. 8 more pounds to go!!! Single digits woohooooo! Then cleaned the house. Went with Ronnie to look at a house she is going to buy. I wish it was me, but that will be soon enough. I put-zed around the yard and played in the sunshine most of the afternoon. I barbecued an amazing meal tonight just for myself. I lit a candle and even had some wine. I am celebrating how great life is. Missing mom as it's Sunday and wish she was here to sort the socks and make me have some really cheesy Chinese buffet. I have a huge week ahead of me with 31 clients already booked in. The nutrition work at the spa is fun, loving fitzone as always, most of all loving being at Mike's gym. I fight with Darryl twice this upcoming week. I hope my shoulder feels better by Tuesday. I'm planning to work on my jab and cross at fitzone between clients so I can knock Darryl on his butt this week. My bruises are looking better, my face is healing well. Still realling from watching the fights on Friday. I'm in awe of my athletes especially Akim. He's my fighter from Dover. A tough kid with a tough life. I have to be careful not to make him into my second son. Keeping an eye on my codependent nature. I just love this kid. He won his fight on Friday and was so happy. I cried when he left the ring and his pals (rough kids) surrounded him with praises. He came to me after and thanked me for my training. He likes the way I get into his head and make him believe in himself. If only he could see what I see in this troubled young man. When he was hugging me and thanking me he said "Mac I think you are the only one who see's that I'm any good." It made me think of you know who. I saw so much good in him but he just had to keep it inside where he could protect himself. So sad, but not my problem anymore. Kassey fought on Friday too winning her title. Man I hope I never have to fight that girl. She does full contact like me only she is deadly. Little

Audry fought too. She's all attitude. I think I can take her one of these days. Oh how I love getting the anger out of me. I know mom and dad look down and think I have flipped. Invited Pat to my big match and he freaked going on about me being diabetic. It was kind of funny. If only he knew that life is short and you have to live it to the fullest and let nothing hold you back especially fear of pain. I believe if I let fear control me I'd never leave this house again. The new me does what she needs to do and says what needs to be said. I may get my nose broke or worse yet my heart, but I'll never let pain be it mental or physical stop me from living life to the fullest. I know what I want and I'm going after it with every fibre of my being. Risk more than others think is safe. Failure is never final unless you allow it to be. Hoping to work on my tattoo drawing tonight.

Gotta get busy, 3 more diets to write. Life is good!

CHAPTER 16

I dare to dream of a better world.

The summer went by quickly as I filled my time with fighting, weight lifting, and working. I managed to get the Evil One removed from my gym by late August. It helped as the anger inside me started to subside. I stopped taking sleeping pills and tranquilizers. I continued to always be on the lookout and maybe always will, but now when I see his truck, my pulse does not rise, and I don't let the fear impact me. At long last, I have gained control. I don't get angry or cry or feel guilty about his mental illness.

I still get texts but only a few per week, and I never respond. People still tell me about his little antics, but I just walk away or change the subject. He hasn't changed, but I have finally accepted that he never will, and this will just be my life. There's been peace in that for me.

I don't even respond when his daughter calls because her dad has taken yet another round out of her. I have told her countless times to call the police and feel there is nothing more I can do to protect her. That is a huge step for a codependent. I am just grateful that one of my children will not ever make that call. Somehow, I came out of this in one piece and maybe even better for it. It's been hard, but I've learned that this doesn't make me cold and uncaring; it makes me wise.

At first I learned that a codependent can get into very unhealthy relationships due to their need to caretake. That was the first step, but I've learned that there is a second step. It's OK to be a codependent. We aren't stupid or bad. I have had to learn to stop and care for myself, not just everyone else. I needed to let my loved ones fall down once in a while and shouldn't always be there to prevent that. I needed to prioritize who I pick up when they fall down. And most importantly, I needed to allow people to pick me up when I fall down, and that's OK. Let me explain for those of you that are reading this in the shelter.

Prior to the Evil One, I had never allowed Mac to fall down. I remember being twenty-two and losing my godbrother in a motorcycle accident. I was devastated but never showed anyone. I never even cried. I spent the first six months after losing him running around, trying to care for his parents and denying all my grief and pain. I denied myself to caretake and developed a huge fear of motorcycles because they were easiest to blame.

When I was hurt in Texas, I chose to blame myself. I didn't allow myself to heal; I had to make up for what I had done to my children and family and, most of all, my new son Branden. The funny part is that I thought I was being strong. I didn't cry.

When I lost my dad, I had to take care of my mom and her farm. I had a few silent tears when I was alone, but I didn't ever ask for a hug or some help because all the people around me didn't need to be troubled with silly little me. I was the rescuer, not the receiver. And I did just that!

When the man I cared for left me for a night with my best friend, I didn't fall apart. I didn't demand an explanation. I actually don't really even know what happened to this day. I just trusted the people that told me about it. I deserved an explanation why they chose to do it on my birthday. I blamed myself because I hadn't been really nice to that man earlier that day because I was upset about cooking on my birthday. I just wrote it all off and went about my business of caring for those around me. I met the Evil One very soon after, and that was perfect because he needed me to care for him.

I didn't go for help when the Evil One and his bipolar antics started. I just kept trying to save him from himself, never realizing that he didn't want to be helped. I kept it all a secret because I wasn't important enough. If he needed to say cruel things or shove me or pull me around by my hair or burn my face off on the carpet or smash my walls in, it was just fine by me. I cried in silence.

When the doctor handed me my tiny dead baby on Easter to hold for a few minutes, I didn't reach out for help. I had terrible cramps for days but worked the next few as if nothing took place. I didn't want to trouble anyone with my failures. I went alone, except for Mom, to the farm to bury his things and spread his ashes. *How stupid is that?* I can ask only myself. That's how I felt stupid and unworthy.

I didn't even ask for help when I got to the women's shelter. I curled up in fetal position and slept for three days. I didn't want to bother the counselors when they had so many others who actually needed them. I thought I was strong and didn't need help. I then went around the shelter trying to help those poor ladies and vowed to build a gym for the poor teenage boys I met (still working on that).

As they unplugged my mom's life support only a few weeks after my son died, I called for my ex-husband so he could help me get my children through this terrible time. I never went to anyone for even a hug. I just worried about my brother and my kids.

Those patterns are codependency. When things get tough, we get tougher. Maybe we work harder. Maybe we exercise more. Most often we find someone in more trouble than us to go help.

I wish it hadn't taken me forty-two years to learn this about myself, but better late than never. If any of this sounds like you, I hope my story inspires you to reach out. You're not being selfish when you ask for help. You deserve it and, better yet, need it.

It's hard to say how it all started with me. I was adopted at ten months old and always felt grateful that someone took me in and always wanted to be good so my parents would never regret their decision, so maybe I had this at birth. I also know I will always have it. I have learned what triggers me and try to stay on track with it.

I have continued to work as a personal trainer because it feeds my codependency. I like helping others; it's my nature. I work passionately with each and every client. *But* when the day is done, I go home and leave them behind. The old me would have phoned each client at every meal to make sure they didn't eat the wrong food. I'm not going to worlds this year as a powerlifter. My body hurts, and it's tired from eighteen months of heavy training. No gold medal is worth dealing with the Evil One. I have learned limitations. Crazy as that sounds, it's a breakthrough for me. I continue to do my Muay Thai kickboxing; however, I only allow myself to train two hours a week. It has meant delaying my first fight, but that's OK; my body hurts, and I need time to heal. I'm not eighteen (wow, was that hard to admit).

I have learned that sometimes I can fall down and cry, and it's OK. In fact it's normal. Only a select few have read this entire manuscript, but I have shared my codependency with three very close friends, and I asked them to keep me in check. Ronnie, who just loves me no matter what crazy things I do; Terry, who got me into the shelter in the first place; and Heather, who is never afraid to speak her mind, but now I will listen.

I don't date, but I am trying. I'm trying to trust. I'm trying to have feelings like I used to. I have learned that this all takes time and unlike the old me, the me before the Evil One, I'm careful now. I have to think about myself, and that's OK!

Journal entry:

Sept 3

7 mos today since that fateful day and at long last I can take a deep breath and just stop. I have 2 trainers starting to replace me next week. I never plan to work over 40 hrs a week again. I train no more than 2 hrs a day. I take every fourth day off my training. I stop and sit still for 1 hr a week. I'm not the scared as much as I used to be or as angry. Got a sad text from the evil one an hour ago but didn't respond. I used to think he would get better but he won't and that's ok.

I miss my mom and dad and that makes me cry. I wish they were here because I need a hug a big hug a long hug. A hug that's all about me!

I don't know who I am anymore but that has to be an improvement. Working hard on taking care of me. sometimes I wish someone would come to my house and climb in my bed and just hold me. Someone expecting nothing, but in the mean time I will hold myself instead. Soon I'm going to do another vision board and have dreams and plans for my future. Safe balanced dreams that are all mine. Maybe I will have a husband one day and yes I will be his caregiver but he will also be mine, and win a kickboxing match. Maybe I will powerlift in Vegas at Olympia (screw the gpc federation) . . . then again maybe I'll go to Africa and help the women in congo. Who knows but somehow I'm on my way back I can feel it.

CHAPTER 17

Two years have passed.

I have just finished the manuscript. I'm sitting in a new home now. I live part time in Calgary and part time in Maui. I'm just in the process of buying my first American home where I hope to retire. Life is very good. Far brighter than pink, and perhaps now, I have a whole rainbow.

I miss my parents, but I don't miss anything else. My Mikayla is busy working on her doctorate degree, making me so very proud. My grandson Able has had his second birthday and is perfectly healthy although he terrorizes his sister Trena, now five. Paige and Kale are doing well and the best parents I know. My Mandy is almost finished with high school. She attends a performing arts school, I hope, not because of all the drama she had watched growing up. Branden is eleven going on twenty. He's very protective of me; he has amazing grades and is the apple of my eye.

Whatever happened to codependent Mac, you may ask? I'm still a trainer and probably always will be. It's a healthy outlet for me due to my former codependent ways. I have five trainers who work for me, and I love them all, wish they needed me more, but once I learned to break some bad habits, they became very independent. My business has been running itself as I write the final draft to this manuscript.

I'm in love with an amazing man. A healthy man. A stable man. He made me breakfast today, and some days I make his. I get to take my own phone calls. I speak my mind with no fear of being hurt. He doesn't think I'm too fat or too thin; he loves me because I'm me. He doesn't need to be rescued. He already rescued himself years ago, just like I did. If he falls down, I can chose whether or not to pick him up, and he can chose to do the same with me. It amazes me how he lets me read each chapter as I finish. He sits and patiently listens to the drama that unfolded, never getting mad, only loving me. Some days he even cries when he hears the stories.

He has taken me to a power lifting meet recently, and we faced the Evil One together, hand in hand. Some days I feel like with Levi at my side, anything is possible. I can't imagine it ever being possible to thank him for his tremendous support as I put closure to my codependency. I had no idea I could ever be this happy.

I had to write this and share this story in hopes that it might help even just one person, and maybe it's you. My dream is that it will be available for every new person that arrives in a shelter. I believe if someone had shared this with me, it would have helped immensely. Somehow, if it were to save one person from going back to their life of chaos, every nasty name I have been called would have been worth it. So I guess in summary, what I have been trying to say is, no matter how worthless you think you are, reach out and get some help. There is a better life waiting. You just have to get out first. You're not alone even though you may feel that way. Tiny steps forward is the perfect place to start. Allow yourself to think about you—that doesn't make you bad. I guarantee someone loves you because you're loveable.

I don't know you and probably never will. Understand that I pray for you. I know you better than you think. Set boundaries every day. Get some sleep. With each passing day, you will get stronger and life will get better. It won't happen overnight, and you'll have little setbacks. It took me a very long time, but you're worth it just like I was—right?

I love you,

MAC

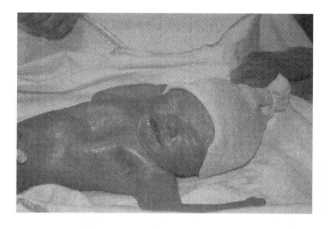

My grandson Able, born nine weeks early.

My mom, 1937-2009.

Kickboxing promo card, 2009.

My children, December 2009.

My children and some of my new family, who seem to love
me and accept me.

The happiest day of my life was on February 14, 2012. I was married on my favorite beach in Maui. I call it my happy place. My precious Levi is neither superman nor a monster. He comes with his own set of issues just like the rest of us. This is the new MAC who knows boundaries and has a wonderful husband who loves her and she loves back!

One in three women will experience

domestic violence.

Get involved.

Made in the USA
Lexington, KY
03 January 2019